CLOCK WISE

CLOCK WISE

George M. Bowman

100624

Fleming H. Revell Company
Old Tappan, New Jersey

All Scripture quotations not otherwise identified are from the King James Version of the Bible.

Scripture quotation identified LB is from The Living Bible, Copyright © 1971 by Tyndale House Publishers, Wheaton, Illinois 60187. All rights reserved.

Library of Congress Cataloging in Publication Data

Bowman, George M., date
   Clock wise.

     1.   Christian life—1960–
I. Title.
BV4501.2.B683   248′.4   78-26844
ISBN 0-8007-0987-X

TO Shirley, my wife, who long ago
did what I hope every reader of this
book will do: She discovered that an
ordered life is a happy life.

Contents

Introduction:
The Image of God

When man was created in the image of God, he was endowed with certain aspects of the divine character and personality. Therefore, God being the essential Planner of all ages, each of us must have been given the ability to plan. Theologians tell us that the image of God in man consists (among other things) of his psychical powers (those faculties which make him a rational and moral being), that is, in his intellect and will, with their different functions.

While it is true that the image of God in man suffered from man's fall into sin, that image was not destroyed, as some are prone to believe. For example, after the Flood, the Lord told Noah that murder must be followed by capital punishment, because murder was an attack on the image of God (Genesis 9:6). In the New Testament, the Apostle Paul, in his first letter to the church at Corinth, said that a man ". . . is the image and glory of God . . ." (1 Corinthians 11:7). And James said that men ". . . are made after the similitude of God" (3:9).

Like all other aspects of the image of God in man, the ability to plan, though not destroyed, was seriously affected by sin. Today, therefore, we find it impossible to fashion a perfect plan for our lives, our work, and our time.

That fact must be understood at the outset of any book that purports to tell Christians how to plan their time. Recognizing that we have no perfect plan, we are driven to seek help with our planning from Him who declares the end from the beginning (Isaiah 46:10).

While God has not seen fit to reveal all the secrets of His planning methodology, He has disclosed enough to leave without excuse those who refuse to plan their lives and behavior. These two important truths were transparently declared by Moses when he said, "The secret things belong unto the Lord our God: but those things which are revealed belong unto us and to our children for ever, that we may do all the words of this law" (Deuteronomy 29:29).

The Bible also shows that God has plans by which He sets goals, states policies, installs procedures, fashions tools, selects personnel, delegates responsibilities, and states times for completion. And nothing is more evident throughout the Word of God than this: Believers are responsible for what they do with their time. "Walk in wisdom," said Paul, ". . . redeeming the time" (Colossians 4:5). We are not to take our lead from modern thinkers who seek to exalt man and his ideas and who give God a very small part in the affairs of this world.

The purpose of this book is to call us back to the One who planned, created, and maintains the universe—the One who engineered all the intricacies of the complex plan to redeem the lost. As members of His redeemed family, through the doing and dying of Christ, let us never forget that God, who is omniscient in His planning, is omnipotent in His performing. We should also remember that His planning and performing extend to the very time that each of us has at his disposal. In spite of the efforts of men to live longer and to eliminate the aging process, the Bible says that God has planned the amount of time He intends to allot to each person's life. For instance, the psalmist prayed: "Thine eyes did see my substance, yet being unperfect; and in thy book all my members were written, which in continuance were fashioned, when as yet there was none of them" (Psalms 139:16). In a similar prayer, Job said that man's ". . . days are determined, the number of his months are with thee, thou hast appointed his bounds that he cannot pass" (14:5).

In view of these indisputable facts about God and life and time, why is it that we still so often try to play God in the area of our planning? Instead of seeking the divine plan for our lives, our work, and our time, we set up plans of our own making. With even a modicum of common sense and the Word of God before us, we should readily see that such plans are doomed to failure.

Our plans are easily frustrated by accidents, mistakes, bad timing, weak and/or dishonest personnel, and other obstacles. But God's plans include all of these so that even the wrath and wickedness of men are made to praise Him. For example, the worst crime in history—the murder of the Son of God—though perpetrated by evil men, was committed ". . . by the determinate counsel and foreknowledge of God . . ." (Acts 2:23). Why, then, should we be so foolish as to be satisfied with our own plans, when we can go to the infallible Word of this great Planner and learn from Him?

To learn from God does not mean that we are to copy the divine plan, for such an attempt would also be playing God. But we can study the rules that the Lord has given us on how to govern our lives, and then we can do our best to implement them as the plan for our work and time.

If this book helps you to plan your life and work and time in such a way that you'll enjoy a closer walk with God the Father, who planned redemption, with God the Son, who purchased it, and with God the Holy Spirit, who applies it to us, my prayer for you will be answered. And may the Lord enable you to ". . . rejoice before the Lord thy God in all that thou puttest thine hands unto" (Deuteronomy 12:18).

CLOCK WISE

1

The Nature of Time

The importance of time is pointed up in the psychiatrists' belief that a person who cannot identify time is childish and disoriented. For example, when you were a child, even if you were highly intelligent, the chances are that you were unable to utilize time tenses (past, present, and future) until you were four years of age. According to the *Encyclopedia of Human Behavior,* a child usually cannot name the day of the month until he is eight years old.

That kind of thing is all right for a child, but when we grow up, we ought to have a more mature understanding of time and the role it plays in our lives and work. ". . . When I became a man," said the Apostle Paul, "I put away childish things" (1 Corinthians 13:11).

But putting away childish things about time is not as easy as one might suppose. For one thing, the whole idea of time is very difficult to define. The *World Book Encyclopedia* says, "It is hard to tell exactly what time is." Then it attempts to do so by saying, "Time is one of the dimensions of the physical universe in which we live."

Nearly sixteen hundred years ago, when Augustine was asked for his definition of time, he said, "If nobody asks me, I know; but if I were desirous to explain it to someone that should ask me, plainly I know not." And the more you look at the subject of time, the more you realize that here is an elusive subject that requires your utmost concentration to understand it enough to put it under control.

Almost everywhere you look, you find attempted definitions that offer no help at all in your quest to manage your time. For example, the *Thorndyke Barnhardt Dictionary* says that ". . . time is all the days there have been or ever will be; the past, present and future," and then goes on to give nineteen subordinate definitions—none of which offers even the glimpse of a clue about time management.

It seems as though everyone is supposed to know what time is, so there's not much mention made of what it really means. Some books you would expect to deal with time don't even mention it at all. For instance, the other day I looked through the indexes and tables of contents of the books on management I have in my library and discovered that fourteen of them carry no reference whatever to *time*. Can you imagine that—fourteen books with titles offering to show readers how to be better managers—with no reference pointing to time and how to use it? Perhaps the authors have discovered, as I have done, that time is not easily defined.

It's not that time is neglected in literature or in conversation. Much has been written and said about time, but like the weather, it is often viewed as beyond our control. Mark Twain's famous quote about the weather is equally applicable to time. "Everyone talks about it," he said, "but nobody does anything about it."

Could it be that we have fashioned in our minds a false concept of time and thus have squeezed ourselves into a limited pursuit of excellence in time control? For example, when we speak of time, we use phrases that are largely untrue. We say, "Time will tell," when we know that time can't speak. We say, "Time flies," when we are fully aware of the fact that time never changes its pace of sixty seconds to the minute. We say, "I don't have time," when it is perfectly obvious that each human being is endowed with the same amount of time each day.

"We all have the same sized pie—24 hours each day," says counselor Jay Adams. "Everything depends upon how you slice it."

Some like to think of time in a philosophical way and so describe it as "one way of measuring vast distances of space." Others like to be obvious, with a slight touch of mystery, so they speak of time in words like those of T. S. Eliot: "Time past and time present," he said, "are both perhaps present in time future."

Then there are those thoughts of time that make us feel guilty, portraying its passing without notice as the source of some kind of self-betrayal or public disloyalty. Thomas Wolfe, the novelist who wrote himself to death before he was thirty-eight, once said, "I did not know what I had done—I only knew that I had ruinously forgotten time, and by so doing had betrayed my brother men."

Of course there's an authoritative view of time which describes it as "the dimension in which things change" or as "the element in nature that causes change." Novelist Faith Baldwin, who wrote many light, sentimental stories for women, once said, "Time is a dressmaker specializing in alterations."

All of these definitions and ideas about time, however, leave out the fact that time is one of the three elements introduced by God in the creation of the universe. Those three elements are space, matter, and time. Mentioned in the first verse of the Bible, each of them is given equal importance: "In the beginning [that's time] God created the heaven [that's space] and the earth [that's matter]."

Throughout the other twelve acts of creation (light, skies, water, land, vegetation, sun, moon, stars, fish, fowl, animals, and man), time is continuously mentioned as part of the creative process: "And the evening and the morning were the first day" (Genesis 1:5. *See also* Genesis 1:8, 13, 19, 23, 31).

The importance of time in creation is explained by Nathan R. Wood in his excellent book, *The Secret of the Universe*. There he shows that the space-matter-time universe reflects the triune nature of God and that time is a vital part of that reflection in its own triune structure of past, present, and future. He also points out that it would be impossible to understand time apart from space and matter.

Albert Einstein seemed to support this when he said that time and space cannot be considered apart from each other, but that they depend upon each other. In other words, the very structure of the universe depends upon the three pillars of space, matter, and time.

Knowing about this is very important, because it shows us that we don't set out to manage time per se, but we must think of time as being related to space and matter. You see, it would be impossible to manage or control time apart from some control of what we do with the material things in our lives and with the space in which we operate. Wood brought them together in this meaningful sentence: "Everything we see, hear, or touch, is known to us through the time length of its vibrations."

It is through time, then, that we experience life and learn everything we know. Benjamin Franklin once said, "Dost thou love life? Then do not squander time, for that is the stuff life is made of."

How foolish it would be to ignore time, "the stuff life is made of," and allow our lives to be lived in chaos and end in ruin! God has created time and decreed that each one of us should be given a certain amount of time to glorify Him, that we might enjoy Him forever. That divinely allotted time will run out almost before we know it. So we must face the fact of the brevity of life if we are going to be successful at managing that time. In chapter two we will look at how short life really is and what we should do about it.

2
Life Is Like a Shadow

The law of supply and demand, that basic law of economics, says that whenever a commodity falls into short supply, its demand and value rise accordingly. That law should be applied to time, because the evidence is overwhelming that each one of us possesses that commodity in short supply. For example, I'll never forget the shock I received when I first learned that a man must do his whole life's work in twenty-five hundred weeks! "That's only twelve thousand five hundred days," I said, "or one hundred thousand hours!" These figures are based on five eight-hour workdays a week, for fifty years. When you consider that most persons don't work anywhere near a total of fifty years, those weeks, days, and hours represent a rare and valuable commodity indeed.

How little time there seems to be for us to do the things we want to do. It doesn't require much of a mathematician to realize that when it comes our time to die most of us will leave behind some unfinished work. For instance, when Raphael, that great Italian painter of the sixteenth century, died, his unfinished painting of the Transfiguration was carried in the funeral procession, as a symbol of the unexpected brevity of life.

Moses knew something of the shock that comes with the recognition that life is short.

> . . . We spend our years as a tale that is told. The days of our years are threescore years and ten; and if by reason of strength they be fourscore years, yet is their strength labour and sorrow; for it is soon cut off, and we fly away.
>
> Psalms 90:9, 10

When we will fly away, we can't know for sure; but life-insurance actuaries tell us that there is a formula for gauging, on the average, what a person's life expectancy is at any age. That formula works like this: Deduct your present age from 80, then multiply your answer by 7 and divide the result by 10. For example, if you are 48 years old, here's how you arrive at your life expectancy:

$$80 - 48 = 32$$
$$32 \times 7 = 224$$
$$224 \div 10 = 22.4$$

It makes one think of the pessimist's view of life: "If I am so soon done for, what in the world was I begun for?"

Perhaps the knowledge of life's brevity was intended by God to make us more dependent upon Him. Looking at those few years we have left, we feel like crying, "Oh, the instability of life!" Is that what David was talking about when he penned these words? "Lord, make me to know mine end, and the measure of my days, what it is; that I may know how frail I am" (Psalms 39:4).

We don't have to live very long before we feel the pressures of the frailty that David spoke about. It touches us all. Shakespeare would have been more accurate, I think, had he substituted the word *humanity* for *woman* and had written, "Frailty, thy name is humanity!" While each age has its own compensations, there is nothing so pathetic as to see a strong man being subdued by the passing of time. Compare, for example, the last photograph of Winston Churchill with that great portrait by Karsh of Ottawa, which was taken when the British wartime prime minister was at his best.

In his book, *The Seasons of Life,* Paul Tournier says, "The further on we go, the more we see time as a diminishing capital."

How easy it is to fall into the lament of our pessimistic friend who wondered what he was "begun for" because his life was so short. One of the psalmists had a similar experience. Looking to the Lord in prayer, he cried out: "Remember how short my time is: wherefore hast thou made all men in vain?" (Psalms 89:47.)

There are some, of course, who never think of the value of their time. Seemingly unconscious that death is just around the corner, they set out deliberately to waste as much of their time as they can. James Henley Thornwell, noted American theologian of the nineteenth century, obtained a lesson in this truth during a sea voyage he had taken to restore his health. In his journal of May 30, 1841, he wrote:

> I was much struck with the various efforts of my fellow passengers to while away the time. Though they would have shuddered at the thought of death, they evidently had more time than they knew what to do with. They tried cards, and dice, and chess; they would walk, and yawn, and smoke, and loll; and, after all, sigh out in awful moans under the intolerable burden of too much time.
>
> Ah me! on a dying bed these wasted hours will be like fiends from hell, to torture and harass the burdened soul. How important is the caution of the Apostle, "redeeming the

time!'' Mark that word, redeeming. It implies scarcity; it teaches that time must be *purchased;* but who, until a dying hour, now finds time scarce, or feels constrained to buy it?

Perhaps it is because men know that life must end that they seek to fill up their time with what they call pleasures. Could it be that they do so to force themselves to forget the obvious fact of inevitable death? The Preacher of the Book of Ecclesiastes put it this way: "For the living know that they shall die: but the dead know not any thing, neither have they any more a reward; for the memory of them is forgotten" (Ecclesiastes 9:5).

The Apostle Paul even warned about putting too much emphasis on the pleasures of married life, because ". . . the time is short: it remaineth, that both they that have wives be as though they had none" (1 Corinthians 7:29).

Though time moves at the same pace of sixty seconds to the minute, as we get older it seems to pass away faster and faster. We stand at the threshold of a new year and say, "Where did the past year go?" Often we feel like the woman who said, "Tain't like there was time any more like there used to be. Even with all these fancy new clocks, time is mighty scarce."

Those of us who believe the Bible to be the last court of appeal on any subject it mentions are convinced that time is not only scarce and that each person is shortly going to use up his or her allotment but that time itself is going to disappear forever. "And the angel which I saw stand upon the sea and upon the earth," wrote the Apostle John, "lifted up his hand to heaven, And sware by him that liveth for ever and ever . . . that there should be time no longer" (Revelation 10:5, 6).

Our knowledge of these things should move us to cry out, as Moses did about his people, who had forgotten where they had come from, why they were alive, and where they were going: "O that they were wise, that they understood this, that they would consider their latter end!" (Deuteronomy 32:29).

Our Lord Jesus Christ is the great example of one who understood the value of time, and how important it is to consider one's time of death. When He sent His disciples into the city to prepare for the Last Supper with them, He told them to speak to a certain man and say, ". . . The Master saith, My time is at hand; I will keep the passover at thy house with my disciples" (Matthew 26:18).

Some argue that such a view of life is too serious and that it takes all the joy out of living. Some even argue that life is too short to be bothered about such deep subjects as death and immortality. "We don't live long enough," George Bernard Shaw once argued, "to take life seriously."

But that is the greatest tragedy of our times: Men and women refuse to recognize the awful truth that "life at best is very brief, like the falling of a leaf." They will not accept the many warnings in the Bible that liken life to a shadow, to a disappearing vapor, to withering grass, to the wind, to a weaver's web and shuttle, to a handbreadth, and to messengers in a hurry.

In his giant novel *Centennial,* James A. Michener tells of a selfish character who, when he came to the evening years of life, had "only one concern: to live past his 70th birthday. And he took every possible precaution to see that he did so." But all his precautions were for naught, and he suddenly took ill with a heart condition and pneumonia and died.

Along with the understanding that death is really not far off, we should learn to accept the life we receive. We cannot change it, and to worry about it is to waste time that could be used for a more profitable undertaking. Richard L. Evans, a syndicated columnist, once wrote these words of common sense:

This is the life in which the work of this life is to be done.
This is what we came here for—even if it isn't what we think

it ought to be. This is it—whether we are thrilled or disappointed, busy or bored! This is life—and it is passing. What are we waiting for?

Some people have a hard time making up their minds, and their indecision wastes valuable time. Like Mr. Micawber, the character in Charles Dickens's *David Copperfield,* they are always waiting for "something to turn up." Time is of little value to such people. What a difference in the attitude of Moses, as shown in this prayer: "So teach us to number our days, that we may apply our hearts unto wisdom" (Psalms 90:12).

How tragic that so many feel it's a waste of time to think seriously about the most important subjects in the world. Talk to them about how to get right with God, how to get victory over sin, and how to escape divine judgment and get to heaven, and they'll respond as the governor Felix did when spoken to by Paul: ". . . Go thy way for this time; when I have a convenient season, I will call for thee" (Acts 24:25).

Apparently he had never read the Book of Ecclesiastes, in which the Preacher wrote, "To every thing there is a season, and a time to every purpose under the heaven" (3:1).

Though the brevity of life is true, we are not to allow that truth to depress us in any way. Such knowledge should urge us on to do greater things for God. Charles Spurgeon, in his *Lectures to My Students,* illustrates the shortness of life by describing a poor seamstress, with her little piece of candle, stitching away to get her work done before the light goes out.

"I must work the works of him that sent me, while it is day: the night cometh," said Jesus, "when no man can work" (John 9:4). He also said, ". . . Walk while ye have the light, lest darkness come upon you: for he that walketh in darkness knoweth not whither he goeth" (John 12:35).

There is no greater darkness than the darkness of ignorance, especially ignorance of the fact that life is too short to waste in idleness or empty pursuits. Harold Nicolson, a wartime British MP in Churchill's government, once described life as "time rushing down the drain." But a drain's purpose is to take away useless waste. Is that a proper view of God's gift of time? Is it nothing but useless waste?

Time is a commodity of such high value that we can't afford to lose it down the drainpipes of wasted efforts. If we learn this early in life, we'll not be forced, in our old age, to make up for time lost in our youth and middle years. For example, Shakespeare's Macbeth came to the end of his ambitious, cruel, and murderous life with a strong desire to justify a life of wasted time. Going out to face Macduff and possible death in battle, he cried out:

> I 'gin to be aweary of the sun,
> And wish the estate o' the world were now undone.
> Ring the alarum-bell! Blow, wind! come, wrack!
> At least we'll die with harness on our back.

But dying with harness on one's back never justifies a life of wasted time. And neither does scurrying around on Friday and Saturday justify a week of poor effort. When I was a sales manager, it used to pain me to see men who had spent the week "swinging the lead" trying to round up some sales on Friday and Saturday.

It's the same in any profession: Imagine a pastor trying to complete his week's visitation on Friday night, or a housewife trying to get all her work done on Saturday afternoon, or a Sunday-school teacher waiting until late Saturday night to prepare his lesson from the Word of God, or a writer trying to meet a deadline by waiting until the last day!

When time is planned, how much better goes the day and the

week! And if we take advantage of the odd moments that usually go to waste, how much more work we can get done. Think of the time you've wasted sitting in a doctor's waiting room or waiting for a bus or waiting for a phone call or for the gas-station attendant, or for an incoming plane or train. All that time could have been profitable, if you had taken along something to do during those waiting moments.

For example, why not make up a "waiting kit" to take wherever you go? In it you could put a notebook, a pen or pencil, a book you want to read, a lesson of a home-study course, some sewing or knitting. I have acquired most of my education by taking a "waiting kit" wherever I go.

My wife likes to knit so much that she's never without a knitting bag, and you should see the large amount of knitted goods she has piled up by taking advantage of those odd moments. "I wish," she once said facetiously, "I could knit in church." I think my wife's learned what Jean Bradford meant when she wrote: "You wouldn't throw away loose change from your pocket; don't throw away the small-change time that accumulates in an ordinary day."

Another person who learned the value of odd moments is David Cornwell. While traveling to and from his work each day, on a commuter train in England, he scribbled in little notebooks instead of gazing at the scenery rushing by. When his scribblings were typed, a publisher bought them, and published them under his pen name. They became a best-selling novel. Perhaps you've heard of it: *The Spy Who Came In From the Cold,* by John Le Carre.

I commenced this chapter by telling you that the very brevity of life makes time extremely valuable. I'm going to end it by telling you that you can push that value to incalculable levels by learning how to make right value comparisons—a subject we are going to discuss in chapter three.

3

Right Value Comparisons

Before we get into the subject of this chapter, I want to get your agreement on three points: First, your time is valuable; second, the control of your time is more valuable; and third, the effective control of your time is the most valuable. Now ask yourself these three questions:

Do I really believe my time is valuable?
Am I truly convinced that the control of my time is more valuable than the time itself?
Do I accept without reservation that the effective control of my time is the most valuable of all?

Making value comparisons in all areas of your life is one of the most profitable exercises to increase your own personal worth in any cause you care to embrace. As a Christian, however, that worth will be multiplied many, many times, for the work you do in the name of Christ has an eternal value. In this chapter I want to tell you about some ideas that will enhance the value of your time and work. But before I do that, let's look at some of the wrong views people hold about time and its use.

A businessman who owned property but didn't know his own age was asked, "How is it that you are so ignorant about a subject that most people take great pleasure in knowing?"

"I keep accurate accounts of my rents and what others owe me, for fear of being cheated," the man replied. "But I never worry about my years, because no one can rob me of those."

When Charles Spurgeon heard this story, he said, "Poor man! did he not know that he was robbed of his precious time every day and every hour? It is gone, too, beyond recovery. If a thief steals our money, it is possible we may get it again; but time that is past never returns; life that is wasted is gone for ever. Learn, then, to turn to account every passing hour."

Another wrong view of time is to dismiss small amounts of time as having no value. For example, if you waste ten minutes a day, over the course of a year you have wasted a week and a half. It reminds me of what I once read about leaking faucets. A leak of one drop a second adds up to about two hundred gallons of water wasted each month.

Some people think of their work in terms of coffee breaks, vacations, and sick time with pay. Instead of seeking ways to fill up their time with living activity, they go about creating ways to kill time. But killing time can be a very expensive kind of murder, and, according to the high value that God puts on our time in the Bible, one day the ghosts of the hours we killed will return to haunt us. Someone has advised with tongue in cheek that the best way to kill time is to work it to death.

Far too many persons fail to recognize that the mismanagement of time can lead to the undermining of one's ability to think. Two or three years ago *Christian Herald* featured an article which listed ten ways to scuttle your own intelligence, and six of those ways had something to do with the wrong use of time: Saying "I haven't got time," being too quick to judge an idea, investing time in a lesser project, expecting quick recognition, failing to invest enough time in a project, refusing to invest time in self-improvement.

No matter what we think of him, we must give Jean Jacques Rousseau marks for his bit of wisdom about the use of time. "All that time is lost," he wrote, "which might be better employed."

Perhaps one of the big mistakes our society has made regarding time is the economic changeover from piecework—paying a worker for what he does—to timework—paying the worker by the hour. This changeover, in my opinion, has created a wrong emphasis which implies that just putting in time is more valuable than production. Even salesmen, who traditionally have always been paid a commission on the sales they made, are now being paid for putting in time. Some firms have compromised by paying their salesmen a salary and commission, to keep a little incentive in the contract.

Paying workers by the hour instead of for what they actually produce on the job has led to other wrong views about time and work. For example, deliberate laziness is often practiced because, "If I put in the time, I'll get paid anyway." The corollary of this is "deliberate ignorance," which is often the way of life for the man who feels his time has a dollar value, regardless of what he knows.

Such people make wrong value comparisons and spend half their time wishing for things to which they have no right. Alexander Woollcott once said, "Many of us spend half our time wishing for things we could have if we didn't spend half our time wishing."

Putting a higher value on time than on production has led to the practice of putting on a big front with no back. You see this in the world of marketing and management more than anywhere else. Men in sales and in sales management often go to extreme lengths to maintain their "image" as they call it. Being paid for putting in time at their offices or on their sales fields, they are satisfied to do only what is necessary to maintain the status quo. Planning and building and creative thought are alien to their lives of bluster and bluff.

A management expert, after visiting several offices where such people worked, was asked if he didn't think the men he had observed were industrious. "The only thing they are busy at," he said, "is at saying they are too busy."

Even in church these wrong views of time are becoming more and more predominant. For example, take a look at the length of sermons today compared to their length one hundred years ago. In 1873 Spurgeon preached a sermon of 6,585 words—better than an hour. In 1883, Thomas DeWitt Talmage delivered a sermon of 4,500 words—better than forty-five minutes. In 1904 Alexander Maclaren preached a sermon of 4,300 words—about forty-five minutes. And the people enjoyed what they heard during those minutes.

Today, it's different: People have time, not truth, on their minds when they sit in church. Pastors are told not to go beyond noon on Sunday mornings. Why, some Sunday-morning services don't even get to the sermon before 11:45, and the people get restless if their pastor speaks more than fifteen minutes. I remember speaking at a missionary conference once where the chairman was so worried about his speakers going overtime that he sat on the platform with a look on his face that clearly indicated he wasn't enjoying the conference at all. Surely an attitude toward time that robs us of the joy of hearing the Word expounded is a wrong view of time. Time should not be viewed as something negative, but as an essential positive—the proper use of which will enhance the value of everything we do.

To help us do this, we must recognize that while we live on this earth time is basic to everything we think, do, and say. As Nathan R. Wood says, "In the world nothing is timeless. Time is the essence of everything in the physical universe. This is, by universal agreement, a time universe." He also says that time is a part of the very life of the soul, as space and matter are not. "The mind," he says, "can do nothing at all without consecutiveness, succession of thoughts." Therefore, "Time belongs to the mind as well as to the physical universe."

The passing of time and the act of thinking have something in common: Neither process can be stopped by man. You can't stop thinking, so you might just as well learn how to think great thoughts. As the Apostle Paul told the Philippians, "Finally, brethren, whatsoever things are true . . . honest . . . just . . . pure . . . lovely . . . of good report; if there be any virtue, and if there be any praise, think on these things" (Philippians 4:8).

In the same way, you can't help putting in time. As I used to say to my children when they complained about having to do chores around the house, "You've got to put in the time anyway, so you might just as well choose to do something worthwhile with it."

While you can't stop the process of time, you can record how you spend it. And that's a good way to find out where you've been and where you went wrong in the order of your time and work. Make a record of what you do for an entire week. If you've never done this before, be prepared for a shock.

You'll learn from that one experience that it's far wiser to recognize that how you utilize your time is more important than how many hours you put in on the job. You'll also learn that you can't buck against the ongoing process of time. As Samuel

Johnson once said, "He that runs against time has an antagonist not subject to casualties."

The effective use of time is not determined by how we manipulate time itself, but by the choices of activity we make. It is too easy to make emotional rather than rational choices. While it goes against human nature (because of the negativeness of sin), we must force ourselves to believe and act upon this truth: Doing the things we *should* do is more important than doing the things we *like* to do and those things we are *urged* to do.

Years ago in China a young Chinese scholar went up to a missionary who had just finished speaking in the open air.

"Do I understand you correctly?" he asked.

"What do you understand?" asked the missionary.

"Well," responded the scholar, "here in China we try to teach people what they ought to do, but we find that this often goes against their natural desire to do what they want to do. But if I understand you correctly, Christianity brings the ought to and want to together so that one who believes in Christ will want to do what he ought to do; is that right?"

"I couldn't have explained Christianity better myself," said the missionary.

Wanting to do what we ought to do is the ideal of New Testament Christianity, but how far short of complete sanctification we fall can be ascertained by that record of one week's personal activity. As it is in theology, so it is in experience: Sanctification requires our constant attention, trying to bring together what we ought to do with what we want to do. Robert Browning must have been thinking of this ideal when he wrote: "We have no time to sport away the hours; All must be earnest in a world like ours."

Another good way to enhance the value of your work and time is to face each day as though it were a crisis time in your life. You have no assurance of tomorrow, and you can't change what happened yesterday. Therefore, make the best of today. "If today was your last day on earth," a pastor asked his people, "would you spend it the way you did yesterday?" When facing a crisis, there is need for a no-nonsense approach. Try the crisis-time approach to each day, and I'll warrant that at the end of the first day, you'll be singing: "What a difference a day makes!"

Such an approach will not allow you the indulgence of sleeping in each day or the neglect of early-morning prayer by which you seek God's direction for the day. Once you catch the vision of what a well-planned day can accomplish and how important it is to seek God's face to help you plan it, you'll understand what Robert Murray McCheyne meant when he said: "I ought to spend the best hours of the day in communion with God. It is my noblest and most fruitful employment and is not to be thrust in a corner."

Getting up early in the morning to meet with God has been the practice of most of history's great men of God. The Bible tells us that early rising was the practice of Abraham, Moses, Joshua, Gideon, Samuel, David, Daniel, and Jesus Christ, of whom it is written, "And in the morning, rising up a great while before day, he went out, and departed into a solitary place, and there prayed" (Mark 1:35).

The virtuous woman of Proverbs 31 is described by Lemuel as one who "riseth while it is yet night . . ." (Proverbs 31:15). When I was a boy, my mother used to say, "An hour's sleep before midnight is worth two afterward." And I think that principle can be applied to work: An hour's work before breakfast is worth two at any other time of the day. William Jay, that eminent preacher of Bath, seems to have believed and practiced this.

In his autobiography of 1854, William Jay wrote:

With few exceptions, I have always practised early rising, being seldom in bed, summer or winter, after five o'clock; and this has been with me, not as with some, who say they rise because they cannot sleep; for it has been always an act of self-denial, since I could enjoy more; but I felt a conviction that it was morally right, as it redeemed time and aided duty; and also that it was physically right, as it was wholesome and healthful. How does it refresh and invigorate the body, revive the animal spirits, and exhilarate and elevate the mind! Yet how many are there, and even ministers, and young ministers, not too much qualified for their work, who can sacrifice all this advantage to the lazy, low, debilitating, disreputable influences of a late indulgence in bed!

Another aid to increasing the value of your time and work is to realize what great things can be done in a few minutes. For example, Abraham Lincoln delivered his famous Gettysburg address in less than five minutes, and Napoleon said that he conquered the Austrians because they did not know the value of five minutes. Our Lord Jesus Christ delivered his Sermon on the Mount in about fifteen minutes—a period of time with everlasting consequences!

We should not wait until the end of our lives to learn the value of time, but lay hold of the truth that even a moment can be packed with untold wealth. Queen Elizabeth I learned this truth on her deathbed. There she cried out, "All my possessions for a moment of time!" God is the Creator of time, and He knows how to enable us to pack lasting and influential worth into what we do with a moment of time. Is He not the great Packer who can pack a whole oak tree into an acorn and a volume of truth into a line of Scripture?

The importance of the present was never so clearly delineated than in the words of the Apostle Paul: ". . . Behold, now is the accepted time; behold, now is the day of salvation" (2 Corinthians 6:2).

If we have been blessed with God's salvation and know something of the grace of God, we ought to understand that He is directing our lives and has placed us in the work He wants us to do. Because of that we should not complain about our jobs, but delight in them as doing the work unto God. "If you can't find the work you like," a wise man once said, "learn to like the work you do."

According to the Bible, such attention to one's work or business leads to prominence. When the president of the company I used to work for asked me if I would like to be promoted, he couldn't understand my saying, "You don't have to promote me to keep me happy with my work."

"Don't you have any ambition?" he asked.

I had seen so many men promoted in the company because the company was afraid of losing them that I resolved never to accept such a promotion. So I answered the president, "You don't understand, Jim. I'll be glad to accept more responsibility if and when the executives firmly believe that I'm the right man to handle that responsibility and that the company needs me in the new position."

When I was promoted, the Lord blessed my work to such an extent that three years later I was invited to a banquet to be presented with the manager-of-the-year award. That award came as a surprise to me, because I hadn't any idea that doing one's job to the best of his ability called for any special recognition. Maybe that's what Solomon meant when he said, "Seest thou a man diligent in his business? he shall stand before kings; he shall not stand before mean men" (Proverbs 22:29).

4

Time and Eternity

How easy it is for sinful men to set up false gods to worship! According to Will Durant, author of the monumental, eleven-volume work, *The Story of Civilization,* there are six kinds of objects of worship. These are celestial (stars, moon, sun, and sky), terrestrial (fertility of the earth), sexual, animal, human, and divine. This view is supported by the words of Moses in Deuteronomy 4:15–19, by which he warned the children of Israel not to corrupt themselves by setting up images or likenesses of anything on earth, in the skies, or in the seas. He also warned them not to worship the celestial bodies by which we determine time.

Perhaps we wouldn't call it idol worship, but I wonder what God thinks of the attitude some people entertain about time. For example, Dorothy Dix once said that time is the great solver of problems, the strengthener, the great peacemaker, and the great consoler. Surely those titles belong to God alone and not to a part of His creation. Miss Dix went so far as to say, "How much anxiety, how much sleeplessness we might spare ourselves if only we would lay our problems on the knees of time."

The purpose of this chapter is to show how time and eternity are related, but that relationship has nothing to do with an attitude that worships time itself or attributes to time the essential qualities of deity. To do that is to practice idolatry—an idolatry that must be as offensive to God as was the worship of Moloch, Baal, Ashtoreth, Dagon, or Rimmon, who were idols of Old Testament times. We can also offend God by the way we react to the pain and problems of time, as we experience them in our own lives.

To get the most value out of a plan for our time, we must recognize that the pain and problems of life are valuable parts of God's plan for us. It has been said that pain sensitizes one and improves his power of concentration. This has been proved many a time when sickness has brought a person closer to God and given him a new dedication to the cause of Jesus Christ.

Some people have an idea that they could get a lot more work done if only they were in better health, but some of the best work in the history of man was accomplished by people in pain, in prison, or with severe problems. Le Baron Russell Briggs, a former dean of Harvard, once said, "Most of the work of the world is done by people who aren't feeling very well."

The Apostle Paul had a "thorn in the flesh," but his work was gargantuan in its scope and influence. John Bunyan wrote his immortal *Pilgrim's Progress* while incarcerated in the prison at Bedford. That pain cannot stop creativity was proven beyond a shadow of a doubt by another writer named John. While suffering from a multiplicity of maladies such as constant headaches, spitting of blood, a hemorrhoidal vein (the pain of which was increased to unbearable proportions by an internal abscess that would not heal), intermittent fever, gallstones, kidney stones, stomach cramps, intestinal influenza, and arthritis, he produced the greatest literary work to come out of the Reformation. I refer to *Institutes of the Christian Religion,* by John Calvin.

Ernest Hemingway, the famous American novelist, once said

that a man's creativity will rise no higher than the degree of his personal suffering. While it is nice to go through life without intense suffering, let us never forget that the birth of great works is usually attended by the birth pangs of labor. Perhaps this is what John Patrick was thinking about when he penned these lines for his play, *The Teahouse of the August Moon:* "Pain makes man think, Thinking makes man wise, Wisdom makes life endurable."

None of this is intended to suggest that we should look for ways to increase our pain that we might be more productive in how we use our time. That kind of attitude smacks of masochism—deriving sensual pleasure from physical pain. Such an attitude is not the mark of a wise man or a hero. Dwight D. Eisenhower, the thirty-fourth president of the United States, was once quoted by a *Time* reporter as saying, "Neither a wise man nor a brave man lies down on the tracks of history to wait for the train of the future to run over him."

It is far better to learn from someone else's mistakes than to learn from your own. To learn from your own mistakes is an expensive way to get an education. That old saying, "Experience is the best teacher," should mean that the experience of others is a better teacher than trying to learn from one's own experience. Risk is reduced considerably when we follow an experienced guide through territory unknown to us, instead of trying to learn the way by our own experience.

In chapter three we talked about the importance of the choices we make on how we use our time. Trying to learn from our own experiences is the wrong use of the power of choice. The wrong use of this power has destroyed many an otherwise-useful life. Knowing the awful consequences of a wasted life, how foolish it is to make bad choices about the way we employ our time! William Shakespeare obviously had observed this folly in the people he studied to gather traits for the characters of his great plays. Note the remorse and cynicism toward life held by his character Macbeth:

> To-morrow, and to-morrow, and to-morrow,
> Creeps in this petty pace from day to day,
> To the last syllable of recorded time;
> And all our yesterdays have lighted fools
> The way to dusty death. Out, out, brief candle!
> Life's but a walking shadow, a poor player
> That struts and frets his hour upon the stage,
> And then is heard no more; it is a tale
> Told by an idiot, full of sound and fury,
> Signifying nothing.

The Christian who understands his relationship to God through faith in Jesus Christ should never be pessimistic about life. He should not be affected by Toffler's *Future Shock* thesis, which says that before the beginning of the twenty-first century, ". . . millions of ordinary, psychologically normal people will face an abrupt collision with the future" and that they will be ". . . overwhelmed by change."

Such a pessimistic view is not new. All through history there have been prophets of gloom and doom who have never taken into account that God is still on His throne and that He holds the future in His divine control. For example, four hundred years ago, Louis Le Roy was so worried about the changes of his day that he wrote a book with this title: *Of the Interchangeable Course or Variety of Things in the Whole World.*

Men have always feared change, it seems, but the Bible-believing disciple of Christ should have such profound confidence in the sovereign will and providence of God that he knows—and acts as though he knows—that his heavenly Father is in charge of all time, including the future. He should never view a crisis as being so large that it can cancel what has gone before or mess up what is to come. And no one should wait until he is faced with a life-and-death situation before he recognizes that time is linked to eternity. An example of this kind of thinking was expressed by Colonel Philip G. Cochran, who helped General Joseph W. Stilwell conquer Burma. Closing a briefing of his pilots before takeoff, he said: "Tonight you're going to find out you have a soul. Nothing you've ever done counts now. Only the next few hours. Good luck."

How different this is from what the Bible has to say about the right use of time! Accepting time as an important part of God's creation, the Christian can link time to eternity by a realization that life is short (Psalms 90:12); by learning early in life that he is accountable to God (Ecclesiastes 12:1); by understanding that these evil times require that he be serious about life (Ephesians 5:15, 16); by directing his earthly duties with heavenly principles (Colossians 3:1, 2); and by setting a consistent Christian example before non-Christian associates (Colossians 4:5).

"Time is lent to us to be laid out in God's service," said Abraham Cowley, a seventeenth-century English poet, "and we cannot be too diligent in it, if we consider that time is precious, short, passing, uncertain, irrevocable when gone, and that for which we must be accountable."

The fact that God has created time gives Him the right to dictate how we use it. And we can be no more done with God than we can be done with time. Reverend Volie E. Pyles, in a sermon entitled "The Parable of the Clock" said, "As you set your daily schedule, as you celebrate an anniversary, as you consult a calendar, as you sleep, as you awake—anything that has to do with time in your life has to do with God. Whenever you can put aside time, whenever you can erase time, whenever

you can stop the sun in its orbit, when you can stop the moon or
the earth in their rotations, whenever you can stop the passing of
time, you can be done with God, but not until then."

In Greenwich, England, is located the timepiece of the
world—the Greenwich Clock. That clock is set according to the
sun. We, too, should plan the time of our lives according to the
"Sun of Righteousness," using His standards to measure our
lives, our work, and our time. In fact, we should copy time in its
obedience to its Creator. What an example it is of a faithful
witness to God! In his book, *Biblical Cosmology and Modern
Science*, Dr. Henry M. Morris comments on Psalms 19:1, 2 by
saying: "Throughout all space and time there is an unlimited and
unending witness to God."

That God Himself works with time is shown in the revelation of
His redemptive plan. "For when we were yet without strength,"
wrote Paul, "in due time Christ died for the ungodly" (Romans
5:6). He also wrote, "But when the fulness of the time was come,
God sent forth his Son, made of a woman, made under the law,
To redeem them that were under the law, that we might receive
the adoption of sons" (Galatians 4:4, 5).

While time has great value, we must never put its value at a
level higher than eternity. To do so will lead to keen disappointment with life. The French poet Charles Pierre Baudelaire made
this mistake and died half-insane from long addiction to drugs.
He became so frustrated with life because of his wrong evaluation
of time that he once said, "One must always be drunk, That says
it all, There is no other point. In order not to feel the horrible
burden of time that bruises your shoulders and bends you to the
ground, you must be drunk incessantly."

Rousas J. Rushdoony, in his *The Biblical Philosophy of History*, speaks about this overevaluation of time, leading to disappointment: "When time becomes the primary and determinative

order of reality, then time becomes a disappointment. Demands are placed upon time which can only be met by eternity."

Another link between time and eternity is to accept the fact that God can prevent us from carrying out our plans and that we should bow without reservation to His divine will. Exhorting those who make boastful plans for the future, James wrote:

Go to now, ye that say, To day or to morrow we will go into such a city, and continue there a year, and buy and sell, and get gain: Whereas ye know not what shall be on the morrow. For what is your life? It is even a vapour, that appeareth for a little time, and then vanisheth away. For that ye ought to say, If the Lord will, we shall live, and do this, or that.

James 4:13–15

It was the Lord's will that Jesus Christ should work within the confines of time. This is another proof of His genuine humanity, a necessary qualification of priesthood. "Wherefore in all things it behoved him to be made like unto his brethren, that he might be a merciful and faithful high priest . . ." (Hebrews 2:17). Just before Jesus healed the blind man, He talked about the works of God being made manifest in the blind man and then said, "I must work the works of him that sent me, while it is day: the night cometh, when no man can work" (John 9:4). That phrase, "while it is day," implies that Christ's work was done on earth according to time.

The grandest link of time with eternity, of course, is the privilege of prayer. Doctor Eric Gurr, pastor of Jarvis Street Baptist Church in Toronto, Canada, says that prayer is the Christian's most difficult task and that believers should persevere if they want to be effective in prayer. "Persevere!" he says. "Tell God everything. If you do not feel like praying, tell Him that. Whatever posture you assume with your body, let your heart be bowed before the majesty of the most high God."

Charles Spurgeon said that far too many Christians think they are too busy to pray. "That is a great mistake," he said, "for praying is a saving of time." And Martin Luther once said, "I have so much to do that I would never get through it with less than three hours prayer each day." Even with the heavy burdens of state in the midst of a civil war, Abraham Lincoln used to spend the hour between four and five each morning in prayer.

In addition to prayer, however, God expects us to exercise some effort. Like faith, prayer without works is dead. For example, when Nehemiah knew that enemies had conspired to hinder his work at rebuilding the walls of Jerusalem, he said, "Nevertheless we made our prayer unto our God, and set a watch against them day and night, because of them" (Nehemiah 4:9). Paul taught the same thing when he told the Ephesian believers that they should be "Praying always with all prayer and supplication in the Spirit, and watching thereunto with all perseverance and supplication for all saints" (Ephesians 6:18).

While Christians should firmly believe that time and eternity are related, they should not accept the idea that eternity is somehow wrapped up in time. Henry David Thoreau made this mistake when he said, "As if you could kill time without killing eternity." It would be far more accurate to say, "As if you could neglect the opportunities of time without losing the blessings of eternity."

When we learn how to manage our time and order our lives in the light of the Word of God, we become effective witnesses to the work of God's blessed Holy Spirit in our lives. John G. Whittier captured this idea in his beautiful hymn, "Dear Lord and Father of Mankind," in which he prayed:

Drop Thy still dews of quietness
Till all our strivings cease;
Take from our souls the strain and stress,
And let our ordered lives confess
The beauty of Thy peace.

5

Clear the Desk for Action

When I was taking a course in professional writing from the University of Oklahoma, under the guidance of the late Dr. Walter S. Campbell, he gave his students this bit of counsel: "You must form a habit of steady work. And in order to do steady work, you must surround yourself with conditions which make such work possible."

He knew that a well-organized work area inspires one to work, whereas the opposite leads to indolence. He also knew that it was up to the writer himself to create the conditions which make steady work possible. Knowing that success in any field of endeavor depends upon the ability to manage oneself, he used to tell us that we shouldn't expect to direct others if we haven't learned to direct ourselves in the place where we do most of our work.

Every kind of work has a control center, and that's the place to start organizing for better time management. For most of us it's a desk, and that is why I called this chapter "Clear the Desk for Action." I want you to take a long, hard look at your desk. Are

47

you proud of its appearance? Or is it covered with what's left over from this morning's newspaper, yesterday's unfinished business, a pile of bulletins you intend to read sometime, and a filing tray full of papers that should have been filed days ago?

Some people do not know how to work at a desk, because they have never learned how to handle the mountains of paper that come to them. For example, I once worked with an assistant manager whose desk was literally piled high—I mean about two feet high—with unattended-to papers. The only clear spot on the desk was a space right in front of him, about two feet square. He wasn't accepted as part of the management team; he was just tolerated until the company could replace him.

I learned from watching him at "work" that paper shufflers are not decision makers, and that paperwork can strangle the productive life out of anyone. One of the best rules for handling paper at your desk is one that was once called a million-dollar idea. If you employ it at your desk, it will likely save up to 75 percent of your time. It's an idea that has one exciting thing about it: It works. Here it is: Handle each piece of paper only once.

Every piece of paper (letter, bulletin, memo, telegram, and so forth) you receive should be acted upon without laying it down again on your desk. If it requires a written answer, and you have all the information you need to make that answer, and you have a dictating machine on your desk, pick up the microphone and dictate your reply. If it's a piece of information that you need to read, but do not need to keep, read it and throw it in the wastebasket. If it should be filed, toss it into the filing tray (if you have a secretary) or file it right then and there.

When I say clear the desk for action, I mean exactly what I say. A clear desk is the control center for a busy man—a busy man who gets through a lot of work each day. My friend Mel Martin, president of Melmart Distributors and head of the Shantymen's

Christian Association, once told me that he forces himself to handle only one job at a time. And at any time the papers for only one project are on his desk. I know there are other factors, but that one practice helps in a big way to make Mel one of the most efficient men I have ever known.

Putting off making a decision concerning each piece of paper on your desk wastes a great deal of your management energy. Frances Eisenberg, in her article, "Time and the Writer," says, "The some-day attitude soaks up energy like a sponge." Clear the desk for action, and you'll have more energy.

You can help clear your desk for action if you don't allow it to become a filing cabinet or a storage cupboard for everything but what you need there to do your job. You can make a good start at cleaning your desk by taking each drawer out and emptying its contents on a table, where you can then sort them to see which of those contents (if any) you need to do your job.

Here, for example, is a list of the contents of a typical desk drawer: elastic bands, Scotch tape, rubber stamps and pad, labels, paper clips, letter opener, various pens and pencils, scissors, address book, various notebooks, box of staples, canceled checks, some photographs, postage stamps, Kleenex, a magnifying glass, various keys, receipts, assorted file cards, envelopes, erasers, and a telephone directory.

The man who has those things in his desk might need them all to do his work, but I doubt it. If you're a clutter-bug, strip your desk and put back only those things you use to do your work.

After you've done that, your shiny-clean desk might make you so proud that you'll develop an "executive complex" and spend too much time sitting at your desk. The desk-bound leader ceases to be a leader. So don't stay at your desk and neglect to go visiting to make those necessary calls.

"When I sit here in my study with all my wonderful books

around me and the Word of God before me," my pastor, Gordon Heath, said to me the other day, "I think to myself, *Wouldn't it be lovely to stay here all day?* But I have visits to make, and once I start making them and get into the thrill of speaking to people about their relationship to Christ, I wish I could spend all day doing that."

Another mistake it is easy to fall into when sitting at a clear desk is this: waiting for new trends to arise so that you can take advantage of them. The true executive keeps his imagination alive and accepts it as part of his job to create new ideas and set new trends himself.

Beware, too, of allowing personal interests to eat up too much of the time you should be giving to important issues. Hobbies, personal shopping, long lunches, reading your favorite newspaper, enjoying a second cup of coffee, and light conversation with an associate are all right in their place, but they should not be allowed to rob you of that time you need for planning, directing, and for keeping things under control.

Don't put off cleaning out your desk, because that one act can make a tremendous difference in how you feel and how you work. Putting things off is a dangerous habit. It has been known to lead to the frustration of ambition, the dissolution of happiness, and to death itself. Knowing that chaos and delay go together, clear your desk and get rid of the chaos, so you can work on one problem at a time. You'll be able to face each problem head-on, well equipped to fashion a solution.

All right, you've got your desk cleared for action; what do you do now? Look at the rest of your work area with the aim in view of arranging it for the most efficiency. I'd suggest that you draw up a layout of your office or study or work area to scale (usually a quarter inch to the foot) and cut out pieces of cardboard to represent your furniture and equipment. Make sure that these, too, are made to scale. Now, you can sit at your clean desk with the layout of your office before you and move all your furniture into different locations without straining your back.

If your office has bookshelves, filing cabinets, and another work surface such as a credenza or table, think of them all as extensions of your desk. With that idea in mind, you can then move them around on your layout until you get them into the positions that best contribute to the desk-extension relationship. By doing this, your desk remains the control center from which you can operate every other function in your work area. For example, in my office I have a large desk at one end of the room. It measures three feet by five feet. Behind me is a credenza on which I have dictating equipment. Inside the credenza, on a sliding shelf, stand the large reference and index books I use the most. On the walls of my office are bookshelves holding the most important books of my library. In front of my desk are chairs for visitors. Filing cabinets are to my left, along with a secretarial desk and an IBM typewriter. This can be used by a typist, whenever I need such services, without interfering with my own work. In a small room off the office is a photocopy machine and built-in cupboard in which I store supplies of stationery, file folders, layout sheets for editing, and my camera equipment. On top of the cupboard is a working area with a cutting board and a postage scale.

No one can tell you what you should have in and on your desk, in your filing cabinets, in your storage cupboards, and on your bookshelves. Everything in your work area, apart from works of art, and so forth, should be germane to your work and should be placed in your work area according to how often you use them. But you are the only one who can select the items for your work area.

As a writer, I know what I need within reach, and I make sure those things are there. For example, on my desk is a telephone, a phone number index, a calculator, a calendar, a stapler, a pen stand which has a compartment for memo paper, and a tray into which I can toss items for filing.

I have found that keeping a filing system up to date is a big time-saver. For example, I once discussed the virtues of my filing system with an editor and suggested that he'd benefit greatly from adopting it for his own work. "I would never have time to install such a system," he said. A little later in the same conversation he said to me, "Oh, by the way, I've got a clipping here I want you to see." Then he started opening drawers, shuffling papers around, getting up and looking in his two file cabinets. "I've got that thing somewhere here," he said. After he took half an hour to find it, I said to him, "If that item had been in my office, I would have been able to get it for you in less than half a minute."

Organized files can be worth a small fortune to you, if they are loaded with ideas you can recall instantly for immediate use when you want them. But more on this subject in chapter thirteen. For now, I want you to recognize the value of efficient filing and to stay away from spending time on useless records. Learn to classify the things you file so that you can recognize their usefulness to you in your work. Filing anything else is a waste of time.

6

The Planning Process

Some people are afraid of setting up a plan for their lives. They are not afraid of the plan, but they are fearful of not being able to live up to it. They simply don't like the idea of setting up a standard by which their work can be measured. The Earl of Shaftesbury meant something like this when he said, "The most ingenious way of becoming foolish is by a system."

I still think it is better to have planned and failed than never to have planned at all. One reason is that you can learn from where you went wrong. Usually the failure comes from not taking enough time to plan aright. For example, when frustration occurs right in the middle of a project, you can pin down the cause as one of these five:

Ignorance: the failure to get enough information before launching the project

Unbelief: commencing a project with no real conviction about its value

Unmanageableness: the failure to break a big job down into small, easily manageable tasks

Exhaustion: caused by failing to recognize that creative energy
   has peaks and valleys
Myopia: caused by subjectivism which fails to take an objective
   view of the project

Any of these causes of frustration can make the planner look
like a fool. Consequently, some shy away from any kind of sys-
tematic plan for their work. The wise man, however, learns from
his mistakes and goes back to the drawing board. Victor Hugo
once said, "The day that starts without a plan will end in chaos."
And chaotic is the only adjective to use when describing the
results of unplanned work.

It should be understood here that time is not the problem in a
poorly planned life—it's lack of self-management. While self-
management is a rare quality, it is possible for anyone to make up
his mind to get himself organized. Some persons are very much
surprised at what an organized life can produce.

For example, an Oxford professor who was known for his bad
work habits was pushed and prodded by his associates to work
more efficiently and consistently. They could see that, apart from
his lack of planning, their friend was a man of immense imagination and intellect. This man's closest friend was the late C. S.
Lewis, who thought him a terrible procrastinator. Lewis also nee-
dled and begged him not to be so sloppy in his work. What was
the result of all this prodding? The production of many fine pieces
of writing, two of which are now world famous: *The Hobbit* and
The Lord of the Rings, by J. R. R. Tolkien.

If you are one of those who has had trouble making a success
out of your planning, ask yourself this question: "If I can't succeed with a plan, how can I hope to succeed without one?" The
fact that planning is difficult separates the men from the boys.
The ability to plan is one of the essential qualifications for leader-

ship, and let's face it, everyone can't be the leader. Even one of America's great leaders admitted that he had a tough time planning his work and that he often failed but that the exercise made him a better man. His name was Benjamin Franklin, and here's how he explained it:

> My scheme of order gave me the most difficulty . . . . Though I never arrived at the perfection I had been so ambitious of obtaining, but fell far short of it, yet I was by the endeavour, a better and happier man than I otherwise should have been, if I had not attempted it.

Since Franklin's day we have been blessed with an abundance of instruction on how to manage ourselves, our work, and our time. Some of it has been good, and some of it has been poor. A large number of people, however, still live in the past and will never change because, "We always did it this way." We should learn from the past, but we can't live in it. An Old Testament writer once said, "Say not thou, What is the cause that the former days were better than these? for thou dost not enquire wisely concerning this" (Ecclesiastes 7:10).

Success in any project is to bring the thinking and the doing together. Someone has said that there are two kinds of people who fail: "Those who think and never do, and those who do and never think." The first is a dreamer, and the second is a bumbler. The other day a woman said to me, "My husband is a dreamer. He is always talking about owning his own lavish restaurant. But I know he'll never be a successful businessman, because he doesn't know how to plan, and he doesn't know what to do."

Unfortunately there are many Christians like that. They talk all the time of grandiose schemes that will never get off the launching pad. Such an attitude smacks of arrogance and has no place in a plan for the Christian life. We must be ready to accept the fact that God has the right to change the direction we give to our lives and to frustrate our plan. That is why the Bible gives this bit of advice: "Boast not thyself of to morrow; for thou knowest not what a day may bring forth" (Proverbs 27:1).

When I was giving leadership training to men in the Christian Service Brigade, we talked a lot about planning, because it seemed to be the most problematic area in the whole program. Out of those discussions we developed the following seven steps of a successful plan. We don't claim originality for these steps, because we gleaned them from a mountain of reading in the field of administration and leadership. Here are those seven steps:

Find and state the need or problem
Set a specific goal
Design a procedure to hit the goal
Choose the personnel to carry out procedure
Prepare personnel and tools for line of action
Take the action and set things in motion
Set up a system to evaluate program, personnel, and actions

If you'd like to see a good example of these steps in action, read the story of Joseph's plan to save a people from starvation in an impending famine. You'll find an outline of Joseph's plan in Genesis 41:25–36. In verses 25 to 32 he uncovers and clearly states the problem: God is going to follow seven years of plenty with a seven-year famine. "It shall be very grievous," said Joseph.

He set a specific goal by saying, "that the land perish not through the famine." His procedure was that a fifth part of all produce be gathered during the years of plenty, and then it should be placed under the hand of one who had the ability to give direction. He called him "a man discreet and wise," which means a man who is able to distinguish between the wheat and the chaff, the good and the bad issues, and who is not easily moved by the praise or criticism of others. In fact, the Hebrew word for *discreet,* I understand, can be translated "ability to direct."

When Joseph said, "Let Pharaoh appoint officers over the land," he was suggesting the installation of a system to prepare personnel and tools for a line of action. And when he talked about Pharaoh's men gathering "all the food of those good years . . . and let them keep food in the cities," he was saying in effect, "Take action and set things in motion."

When he suggested that the whole plan be under the supervision of those given authority by Pharaoh, he was suggesting a system by which the whole program, all the personnel and their work, could be regulated and evaluated. What was the result of his seven-step plan? Pharaoh appointed him to head up the plan, and the record says that ". . . the dearth was in all lands; but in all the land of Egypt there was bread" (Genesis 41:54). So much so, in fact, that ". . . all countries came into Egypt to Joseph for to buy corn . . ." (Genesis 41:57).

Please note that Joseph took time to define the problem before he rushed into a solution. Once that definition was clear, he then set up a master plan of things which had to be done and the order in which they were to be completed. The Royal Bank of Canada once offered these four steps for planning:

1. Have in mind what is next to be done
2. Attack the task decisively
3. Resume work readily after an interruption
4. Forge ahead steadily to the end of the job

Those four steps would be better applied to procedures than planning. Planning takes place before you set out to attack the task, to resume the work, and to forge ahead to the end of the job. But I hasten to add that those steps are excellent if used to carry out an assignment from the planner.

One of the great planners of history was the Apostle Paul. His missionary itineraries, his epistles, and his sermons all show evidence of his ability to plan. Apparently he never allowed things that happened to give him much anxiety or to color his thinking when planning the future. Although he had accomplished great things as a Jewish leader, because he had excluded Christ in those accomplishments, he never drew on them to help him plan his work as a Christian leader.

His formula for planning was to forget the past and look forward to his goal, with much attention to the details. Here's how he explained it: ". . . this one thing I do, forgetting those things which are behind, and reaching forth unto those things which are before, I press toward the mark for the prize of the high calling of God in Christ Jesus" (Philippians 3:13, 14).

Perhaps your past is keeping you from becoming a successful Christian planner. Don't give in to such fears. Believe the Bible where it says:

But God hath chosen the foolish things of the world to confound the wise; and God hath chosen the weak things of the world to confound the things which are mighty; And base things of the world, and things which are despised, hath God chosen, yea, and things which are not, to bring to nought things that are: That no flesh should glory in his presence.

1 Corinthians 1:27–29

Who can measure the potential of one human being who has been chosen of God? It would do us good to remember once in a while that God is not limited by our past, our social standing, or our economic environment. For example, Joseph went from prison to the palace; Daniel rose from a prisoner-of-war to the top adviser to the king; Jacob was a fugitive who became a prince with God; Moses, the child of a slave woman, rose to become the deliverer and lawgiver of Israel; and David went from minding sheep to the throne of Israel.

Don't ever limit the grace of God in the life of those who believe in Christ and seek to follow Him. When I was a boy, my family was so poor that all of us had to stop our education before we ever got to high school. We had to go to work to help feed and clothe our family of eleven children. In those days survival was the order of the day, and at the age of twelve I went door-to-door, peddling fish in order to survive.

When I was converted to Christ at age twenty-six, I had no education to speak of, had acquired the habits of drinking and smoking, and could see no future whatever. At the end of my rope, I went to church one morning and surrendered to the claims of Christ. Within six months, my outlook on life had changed entirely from pessimism to optimism, and I was given a position selling educational courses to people employed in the business world. Imagine me, without an education, trying to sell it! But God blessed my efforts to such a degree that in nearly every summer contest I was the top salesman on the North American continent.

In my last six months as a sales manager—just before I resigned to take up Christian writing full time—my team of salesmen led the entire nation in sales. Since then God has led me into the work of editing a missionary paper and writing books as a

ministry to my fellow Christians. Because of all this, I am abso-
lutely convinced that God is not prevented by a man's bad start,
poor circumstances, or foolish mistakes from giving him a position of responsibility in Christian work.

But back to planning and a few more ideas that you can use in
a practical way in your life. If your work takes you outside to call
on others, make it a practice to route your calls so that you don't
cover the same territory twice. This one thing will save you a
great amount of time.

Another way to save time is to force yourself to do the things
you know you must do to carry out a plan. For instance, the other
day I asked a very efficient waitress what was the secret of her
amazing ability to get so much work done in a short time. "At one
time," she said, "I hated this job, so I forced myself into a routine
habit of life, so I could get the work done without thinking about
it. Now I find I enjoy my work so much that I look forward to it
each day."

Her phrase, "a routine habit of life," really took my attention,
for I could see that she was talking about setting up a plan with
such attention to details that her work became a routine. Did you
notice her great discovery? Planned work leads to the thrill of
accomplishment.

I received a similar thrill some years ago, by making a minor
change in the weekly report I required my salesmen to turn in.
The report was designed to show management what each man
was doing: number of calls made, numbers of sales interviews
completed, number of sales closed, volume of business those
sales represented, and the number of new prospects he obtained
each week. Feeling that sales were not what they should be, I
made a detailed study of the salesmen's reports, looking for the
reason or reasons that sales were down. I suggested that we ask
the men for one more piece of information each week. A few

weeks later sales were up, and I got the thrill of knowing that we had done something right. What was that little bit of information we asked for? We simply asked the men to tell us each week how many sales appointments they had lined up for the coming week. To get that information the men had to plan ahead, and that planning operation increased our overall production.

My purpose in suggesting that change was to increase volume of sales for each representative. And that reminds me that the development of any long-range plan should have as its first essential a clear statement of purpose. If it's a long-range plan for a business or an association or a church, ask this question: "What business are we really in?" Making a clear statement of purpose is indispensable to the skill of setting goals—our subject for chapter seven.

7

How to Set the Right Goals

The way some people plan their work reminds me of the boy who took the empty wooden thread spools discarded by his mother and mounted them on a board. They were mounted in such a way, with string running from spool to spool, that when he wound a little crank attached to a spool on the corner of the board, all the spools would turn. Everything was moving, but it wasn't going anywhere. You see, it wasn't linked to any plan beyond motion and pleasure.

The minutes and hours of some people's lives are like those spools. They don't go anywhere, because they are not linked with the rest of their lives. And no one can effectively employ the next few hours if he hasn't planned the next five years. Planning the next five years involves the process of setting goals.

The first step in any effective plan to manage your time is to lay out a piece of paper and write down your major lifetime goals. The list could include such goals as financial security, a more responsible position, a happier family life, more successful church activity, a satisfying relationship with the community, a more fruitful Christian life, good health, a better knowledge of the Bible, a new home, a world cruise, a college education for your children, owning your own business, building the business you now own, or, if you are a pastor, doubling your church attendance.

If you want to be a leader in any area of human activity, you must learn to be a planner who gives direction to that activity, not one who sits around waiting for things to develop. Human nature is so negative that the only things it can develop without a plan are problems. And problems, unchecked, can lead to chaos.

No one can tell you what your lifetime goals should be, but they should be commensurate with your circumstances. For example, a married man would have different goals from a bachelor, a manager would have different goals from those chosen by a missionary director.

After you have written out your lifetime goals, underline the two or three goals most important to you. Go into great detail to describe them and what you think will have to be done to attain them. For example, let's say a major goal of yours is to acquire a good education in business administration. However, you are married, and you have three children, a full-time job, and a home to maintain. In addition, you are an officer at your church, and you teach a boys' Sunday-school class.

It is obvious that you would find it impossible to attend classes to get this education. Therefore, you must resort to home study in accounting, commercial law, management, marketing, and finance. Knowing you can't attend a university, you start looking around for a school that provides the subjects you want in a home-study course.

Next, working with the school, set an estimated time for completion of the course. Once that date is set (say, two years from commencement), you should ascertain how many study hours are needed to complete the course. Then you divide that figure by 104 (the number of weeks in two years) to learn how much time each week you'll need to study. Next, you plan what days of the week you are going to study and the exact time each day you will go to your books. Most home-study students find that early morning is the best.

Breaking down your big goal of acquiring an education into small daily tasks is a sure way (unless the Lord wills otherwise) to guarantee that you'll hit that objective. Most people can't take in the scope of the work necessary to hit a major objective. But reducing that objective to small tasks, each one of which can be completed in a small part of the day, makes big goals acceptable and their attainment quite easy.

Setting goals is a starting point only. You must also add policies and procedures, and you must know the difference between them. A goal, for instance, is a specific objective you desire to attain. A policy is a definite rule to be observed during the process of attaining your goal. And a procedure is an instruction on how to adhere to policies and attain your objective.

Emerson once said, "Our chief want is somebody who'll make us do what we can." While most people must be given direction in life and told what they must do, a leader in society must be the somebody who makes himself do what he can. He must learn to set goals, establish policies, and implement procedures. He knows how to delegate the activity rather than doing it all himself.

Unplanned activity does not produce good results or make for a happy, satisfying way of life. One famous writer once went so far as to praise unplanned activity, especially for young people. "There is a divine irrelevance in the universe," he said, "that defies calculation." He based his opinion on his own experiences as a youth who seemingly wasted his time taking Spanish instead of French, of knocking around Europe and the United States, trying to find out what he believed in and then becoming a very successful writer after he was forty.

He said:

> As a consequence, I have never been able to feel anxiety about young people who are fumbling their way toward the enlightenment that will keep them going. I doubt that a young man . . . is really capable of wasting time regardless of what he does.

The point that author failed to make was this: He never managed to produce anything worthwhile in his life until he settled down to planning his time and activity to the last detail. Now when he sets out to write a book, he spends many months planning, researching, and thinking it through. His reference to a so-called "divine irrelevance in the universe" as an explanation of his own misguided youth seems to me to be a philosophical attempt to justify many wasted years.

Instead of taking his advice, wouldn't it be a lot better to ask yourself, "How would I like to spend the next five years of my life?" To fashion an answer to that question would result in setting goals and relating all of one's activity to those goals. It's the same for a church.

For instance, some churches are so wrapped up in direct evangelistic work that the leaders forget the most important function of the church: to train members to be effective witnesses for Christ. When a church sets the goal of multiplying the number of its members who can readily explain what it means to be a disciple of Christ, think of the wider potential of that church, not only for now, but for the future, when the present leaders have gone to glory!

Of course, there are some who won't set such goals, because

they are afraid of change. But we shouldn't be afraid of any change if it's a change for the better. Others will never be leaders or planners because they don't accept their responsibilities as employees. If we can't learn to follow a plan set by someone else, how can we expect to become planners ourselves? This is so important that I'm going to conclude this chapter by taking a look at why people fail on the job. In a test made by Harvard University, it was discovered that the four biggest causes of men and women losing their jobs were these:

Failure to cooperate
Unreliability
Absenteeism
Laziness

These were followed by troublemaking, drinking, breaking the rules, carelessness, dishonesty, and habitual lateness. If you want to succeed in business or in any other area of endeavor, you will shy away from these negatives and put into practice their opposites:

Be eager to cooperate
Be dependable
Be always on the job (except for emergencies)
Adopt and show an obvious love for your work
Get along with your work associates
Refuse to drink alcoholic beverages
Respect the rules
Always do the best job you know how
Practice unswerving honesty
Always be on time for work

8
Problems With People

The importance of planning your time is multiplied when a major part of your job is dealing with people. Management or leadership is not the skill of sitting behind a desk, signing important papers, but the science of getting things done through people. The Apostle Paul once made the observation that ". . . none of us liveth to himself, and no man dieth to himself" (Romans 14:7). In other words, we are involved with others, and we must recognize that fact. "I want to be alone" is a philosophy that didn't work for movie actress Greta Garbo, and it will not work for the success-minded manager, pastor, or church leader.

We must also accept the fact that where there are people, there are problems, and true leadership is never shocked or surprised when personnel problems arise. Seeking to keep problems to a minimum, the leader sets an example of the formula for greatness taught by Jesus Christ. ". . . whosoever will be great among you," he said, "let him be your minister; And whosoever will be chief among you, let him be your servant" (Matthew 20:26, 27).

The man who wants to be a Christian leader in any realm of life (church, business, education, profession) must learn to adopt the service concept. After all, the real mark of a big man is his willingness to do a menial job for others.

In any group endeavor, the managing must be done by the management. If it isn't, the members of the staff will manage themselves and their work, usually with little or no concern for overall goals.

Because of this, it is vital to the life of an institution that its leaders recognize the main functions of dealing with people. The first function, of course, is to find the right people for the various parts of the process of attaining executive-set objectives. This is so important that you'd be wise to spend more time on choosing personnel than on any other duty. This is especially so when selecting persons to be leaders of others. Every potential leader should be examined for his ability, his behavior and for his creed.

You learn about his ability through a study of his past and by testing him for the skills germane to the job he's being examined for. Behavior can be judged either from observation or from speaking to people with whom the candidate has had regular dealings. His creed is not to be determined by his ability to quote the Bible. There must be evidence that the candidate has convictions that will motivate him in the right direction so far as the position you want him to fill is concerned. A handy tool for this task is a personnel chart. It could be titled "Possible Leaders" and be ruled in vertical columns with these headings: *name, ability, behavior, creed, remarks.* Then, as you satisfy yourself on each heading, you would date the column on the day you receive the information to convince you. The chart should look something like Figure One. Suggested names for this chart would come from your own executive members or church board, who present them along with reasons for making their recommendations.

Possible Leaders

Name	Ability	Behavior	Creed	Remarks

Figure 1

After you have chosen your leader and the people he will lead, you must weld them into a working team. Each must be placed so as to contribute to progress and harmony. For example, look at Moses' experience at trying to lead the people of Israel by himself, especially in the area of judging their disputes one with another. When Jethro, his father-in-law, saw him at work, he said, ". . . The thing that thou doest is not good. Thou wilt surely wear away . . . for this thing is too heavy for thee; thou art not able to perform it thyself alone" (Exodus 18:17, 18).

Then he counseled Moses to set up a system of ordinances and laws to show the people how they should behave themselves and told him to delegate the judicial responsibility of maintaining the system to other men who had ability, proven character, and strong convictions.

> Moreover thou shalt provide out of all the people able men, such as fear God, men of truth, hating covetousness; and place such over them, to be rulers of thousands, and rulers of hundreds, rulers of fifties, and rulers of tens.
>
> Exodus 18:21

Moses had a common problem—one that plagues many organizations—the refusal or inability to delegate responsibility. There is no greater cause of chaos than the head of an institution, a business, or a church trying to run a one-man show. If you would have success as a leader, learn to delegate, for there's more power in teamwork than there is in steam work.

A handy tool to help you delegate responsibility is the delegation chart. Down the left hand side would be listed all the departments of your organization and their functions. Across the top would be the names of your personnel. As the leader, you must take the time to match each responsibility to a member of your staff. This is done by placing an X where the two meet on the chart.

For example, Figure Two is the delegation chart I used when I was committee chairman of the Christian Service Brigade unit in a local church. Using charts, I learned that D. L. Moody was right when he said, "It's better to get ten men to work than to do ten men's work."

Another major function of leadership is to watch for and seek to remove causes of friction between people. Much friction can be prevented by accepting the maxim that one cannot effectively supervise more than six to ten persons. Another prevention is to make sure that each person knows exactly what he or she is expected to do.

These two preventions of disharmony can be implemented if you'll adopt two easy-to-use management tools. They are a job description and an organizational chart. Make sure that each member of your staff is given in writing a detailed description of what the organization expects him to do and a chart showing his place in the organization and the person to whom he is responsible. Figure Three is an example of an organizational chart. If you'll take the time to learn how to prepare and use these in your group, you'll prevent a great amount of potential friction among your personnel.

Warning: Beware of complicated systems for managing personnel. It is the easiest thing in the world for a leader to be so engrossed in charts and ideas that he forgets that he's in the people business. You can avoid this by obeying one simple rule: Keep in touch. In other words, know what your people are doing, and let them know what you feel toward them, even those who work at a distance from you. The Apostle Paul, who was a master at this function of leadership, wrote to his people at Colossae and said: "For though I be absent in the flesh, yet am I with you in the

Delegation Chart

Duties	Delegated to				
					Others

Figure 2

Organization Chart (The Shantymen's Christian Association)

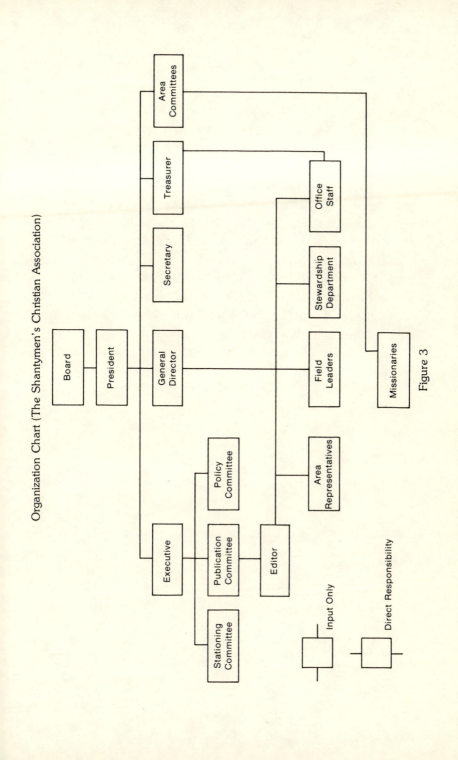

Figure 3

spirit, joying and beholding your order, and the stedfastness of your faith in Christ" (Colossians 2:5).

Paul knew, and so should we know, that leadership requires a just and unselfish attitude, one that does not make favorites, but loves all in equal measure. He also knew that there's no room for pride in the seat of responsibility, for the two do not go together, and that the right attitude toward leadership produces humility. For example, listen to the mighty King David—one of the world's greatest leaders: ". . . Who am I, O Lord God? and what is my house, that thou hast brought me hitherto?" (2 Samuel 7:18) or hear the words of Solomon, the wisest man who ever lived: ". . . I am but a little child: I know not how to go out or come in" (1 Kings 3:7). And didn't Paul, with all his leadership qualities, refer to himself as the chief of sinners?

These men knew that it is a great privilege to be placed into a position of Christian leadership—a privilege with commensurate responsibilities—and that knowledge forced them to a right evaluation of themselves.

9

Use Planning Calendars

Throughout history there have been various ways and means used to measure and control time. These have included a stick and shadow, the sundial, an hourglass, a marked candle, the Chinese water clock, the regular clock, the watch, the radar receiver that can measure time accurately to one thirty-millionth of a second, and electric timepieces which are very accurate because alternating current changes its direction of flow sixty times a second. Then, of course, there are calendars. All of these were invented to help man control his time; but, in most cases, they haven't succeeded. The reason being that such devices cannot help a man to give direction to his work.

If you want to be a leader who gives direction to his work, I suggest that you use planning calendars. These can be set up for a year, a month, or a week. For example, Figure Four is the planning calendar I use to plan a week's work. You can draw up this kind of thing on loose-leaf sheets and keep them in a binder. This time-planning tool will encourage you to plan the details of next week's work this week.

Weekly Planning Calendar

	Sunday	Monday	Tuesday	Wednesday	Thursday	Friday	Saturday
9:00 A.M. TO 12:00 A.M.							
1:00 P.M. TO 5:00 P.M.							
6:00 P.M. TO 10:00 P.M.							

Figure 4

Every Friday, set aside an hour or two to do nothing but plan next week's work. This is the most important time of your week—so important, in fact, that I'm going to repeat myself: *The time you spend to plan next week's activities is the most important time of your week.*

Begin each week's planning session with a review of what you did last week. In this way you can determine where you can improve or change your schedule to get more done in less time.

Now list all the things you have to do. Then list all those things you want to do. Take enough time to list everything: family and social responsibilities, occupational duties and church work, reading and study, banking and bookkeeping, filing and records, recreation and exercise, phone calls and letters—everything. And list them in detail. For example, if you are a pastor, your list, in part, might look like this:

Prepare program for Sunday services
Prepare sermons for Sunday
Prepare Bible talk for prayer meeting
Speak at prayer meeting
Preach two sermons on Sunday
Make up church ad for newspaper
Write church bulletin
Visit sick members
Classify and file ideas
Daily devotions
Plan next week's work
Visit twenty homes in area
Attend deacons' meeting
Spend Saturday afternoon with children
Spend two evenings at home with family
See Sunday-school superintendent

Clean up current correspondence
Prepare Bible-class lesson
Teach Bible class

Please note that time should be set aside for one's family. The busy leader can easily slide into a routine that makes him too busy to spend adequate time with his loved ones. According to the Bible, the man is the head of the family, and it is his duty to give direction to much of the family's activity, especially in the areas of teaching and discipline. The head of the family should also set an example of love and loyalty. For instance, children should be made aware of their obligations to spend time with the family. One of the best ways to teach them this lesson is for Dad to set aside time in which the children have his undivided attention. He can be an example of love by planning special times to spend with his wife, times in which their love for each other is rekindled and enlarged. That kind of love is bound to show and helps to keep a family cemented together.

Once you have made out your list, go over it carefully, writing the name of a day beside each item. The selection of some days is already made for you. For instance, Sunday for sermons and teaching the Bible class, Wednesday for talk to prayer meeting, Thursday for church advertisement deadline, and Friday for planning next week.

Now reorganize your listed duties according to the days of the week. Then take the items for each day and write them into your planning calendar in the order of their importance. This will give you a well-organized picture of what you are going to do next week, with no fussing around, wondering what to do first.

You can do your long-term planning the same way. For a year's planning for example, set up a twelve-space sheet—each space representing a month of the year (*see* Figure Five). Then write in the spaces all scheduled events for the year. If you are a church pastor, these might include the following:

Church annual business meeting
Sunday-school picnic
Young-people's retreat
Outside speaking engagements
Evangelistic campaign
Church-association convention
Visits from guest preachers
Sunday-school contest
Deacons' meetings
All other committee meetings

Such a chart will give you a great feeling. You'll be confident about where you are going and what you are going to do for an entire year! This planning-calendar idea agrees with the maxim that happiness comes from control. Nothing could be farther from the truth than to believe the silly idea that restrictions make for unhappiness.

My wife uses a wall calendar to plan her yearly and monthly activities and a weekly planning calendar (as above) to plan her weekly work in detail. "It's a great feeling," she says, "to know where I'm going, what I'm to do, and when I'm to go and do it."

Another big help in planning your activities is a series of schedules that tell you at a glance those things you should do every day, every week, and every month. These could also be loose-leaf pages in your binder. I keep mine right up front on one page that looks like this:

Planning Calendar for Year

January	April	July	October
February	**May**	**August**	**November**
March	**June**	**September**	**December**

Figure 5

Daily Duties

Devotions (Bible study and prayer)
Writing
Correspondence
Exercise and rest
Editing duties
Filing
Reading and research
Plan tomorrow's work

Weekly Duties

Prepare Bible-class lesson
Bookkeeping and banking
Attend missionary prayer luncheon (Wednesday)
Interview persons for possible stories
Visit office of Shantymen
Plan next week's work
Attend church services
Spend time with family
Teach Bible class

Monthly Duties

Attend board and committee meetings
Make up statement and expense accounts
Missionary trips
Plan work for next month
Complete editing work for current issue
Proofread current issue

These duties should be coordinated into your master planning calendars for the week, month, and year. If you have a natural aversion to a system of control, you should know that only through control will you receive happiness, satisfaction, and contentment in life. For example, in my own experiences as a freelance writer, I am called upon to interview all kinds of persons, some of whom have lived their lives with almost no control. Without exception, each person who had attempted to find happiness by rebelling against moral control was very unhappy. In every area of life where we attempt to live apart from rules and regulations we will create a persistent feeling of unhappiness, until we make up our minds to change our ways.

Ted De Moss, president of the Christian Business Men's Committee, once said that he never really found peace in the struggle of life until he learned from the Bible not to lose sight of his priorities and to adopt a system of control. Using Matthew 6:33 as his guiding principle, Ted says, "My first priority is God; my second priority is my family; number three is my job; and my fourth priority is what I refer to as my ministry." By *ministry* Ted means the work he does for the church and CBMC.

Ted also says that from his observations most businessmen make the mistake of putting their jobs first, their community duties second, their families third, and their personal relationship to God fourth. "I have found," he says, "that priorities aren't in line unless God is put first." The value of priority thinking in a system to manage time is so great that I'm going to use all of chapter ten to talk about it.

10

Establish the One-Two-Three System

As the leader or manager of an organization, you are responsible, not only to plan what's to be done, but to decide the order of work. This is especially true concerning your own duties. While long-term planning is very important, don't make the mistake of downgrading short-term performance. You can be so mesmerized by the long-term goals that you may look upon the daily routine as being of small significance. Like those men of Zerubbabel's day, who couldn't see the importance of the daily work needed to rebuild the temple, you may fall into the trap of despising "the day of small things." It is impossible to perform on a long-term basis. Long-term planning? Yes! Long-term performing? No!

After you have established your long-term plan, you should set the gears of your mind to operate on a day-to-day basis. Remember, it's not your eye on the target, but the way you handle the gun that scores the bull's-eye. Target watching, after all, can be an obstacle to success. For example, a student graduates, not by keeping his eye on a degree, but by getting down to the daily routine of hard study. And a runner wins a race, not by giving all his attention to the trophy, but by concentrating on day-to-day training.

Unless you recognize and adopt this principle of long-term planning with short-term performance, you cannot succeed as a leader. Long-term performance is so enervating that it exhausts the man who tries it. No man alive has enough strength for such an impossible task. That is why Moses wrote ". . . as thy days, so shall thy strength be" (Deuteronomy 33:25).

Now, having established the importance of doing one day's work at a time, let's look at the different ideas that people have for getting through the day. First, here's a general division of the twenty-four hours of the day that might help you to form a practical overview of your day. This breakdown is only a suggestion and is not intended as a hard-and-fast rule to which you must adhere. But it may serve as a guide if you try to divide your day something like this:

Work	8 hours
Sleep	8 hours
Meals and grooming	3 hours
Exercise and recreation	2 hours
Prayer and Bible study	1 hour
Study and self-improvement	2 hours

When setting up such a division, beware of wasting time on nonpriorities. There's no real satisfaction in wasting time, so you must assume that what you plan to do is worthwhile. For example, it is easy to do those things we enjoy and kid ourselves into believing they are worthwhile. This is not to say that enjoyable activity can't be worthwhile. The idea is to study and evaluate all activity concerning its relationship to your previously set, worthwhile goals. Puritan Richard Baxter once gave this rule for evaluating activity: "Spend your time in nothing which you know must be repented of, in nothing on which you might not pray the blessing of God."

One man I know likes to get rid of the routine matters early in the day, "Because it leaves my mind free," he says, "to zero in on the more difficult subjects." Another says, "I like to first do the job that worries me the most, because I can't think clearly while I'm worried."

Some management consultants say that clear thinking comes easier during those times of the day when you are at your peak, when you work best. "All creative work and planning," they say, "should be assigned to such times."

While these three ideas might be helpful to those who propound them, I doubt if they can stand up under universal scrutiny. For example I would never spend the early hours of my day to get rid of routine matters. That's the time when I'm the most alert and wide-awake. I invest that most valuable time of my day into creative writing and leave the routine tasks until later in the day.

I feel the same about the suggestion that one should do the most worrisome job first. Surely the priority of a job should not be judged according to how much it worries me. I find that the allocation of a job to a specific time in my day allows me to forget it until it comes up for attention. The supervisor who wants to succeed as a leader should learn to so plan his time and work that there's no room for worry.

And so far as allowing for peak times in which to plan and do creative work is concerned, I don't think that suggestion can be utilized by everyone. If some of us waited for those peak times, when we are feeling great, we'd never get any work done. Most of the writers I know write every day, whether they feel like it or not.

For example, Dick Perry, author of more than a dozen novels, in his book, *One Way to Write Your Novel,* says, "As I write this I have a combination summer cold and headache, got in late last night, longed to sleep forever, but it is six hours later, and here I sit at this monstrous typewriter . . . ."

If you still think you have to wait until some mysterious peak time of the day to plan or do creative work, go back to chapter four and read the examples used there to illustrate the truth that most of the work of the world is done by people who aren't feeling well.

Many good days are lost, too, by people who allow their anxieties to give direction to their work. Most worrying is about things that have happened or the result of fear of what might happen. The wise leader knows that it is folly to worry about the past, for it can't be changed, and that it is equally foolish to worry about the unknown future. If you suffer from such work-destroying anxieties, here's the cure you need: Give all your attention to the present, and use it to plan and do your work. You'll then discover that your worries will get lost in the dust of your ongoing accomplishment.

Another big obstacle to getting through the day is the failure to make sure that each part of our work gets its fair share of our time. Some executives actually allot so many minutes to each item on the schedule and refuse to give it any more time. I think there's merit in this idea, if you modify it according to your own circumstances. For instance, there are some duties that must be completed today, regardless of what else gets gone, and if they take a little more time than what has been assigned to them, so be it. Priorities have been kept under control. Speaking of priorities, here's an idea on priority thinking that is worth twenty-five thousand dollars.

That's right: a twenty-five-thousand-dollar idea that you can have and use for the small price of reading the next few lines. If you adopt it, I am convinced it will be worth at least that amount to you.

Some years ago, an efficiency expert presented this idea to the president of a large corporation. "Use it for two weeks," he told the president, "and then send me a check for what you think it is worth."

At the end of the two weeks, the efficiency expert received a check for twenty-five thousand dollars. What was the idea? It is so simple that most people will trip right over it, looking for something more difficult to do. Here it is: *Do things in the order of their importance.*

The efficiency expert had explained to the corporation president that he should make a list of his duties for each day, number them in the order of their importance, and then concentrate on the first one, until it was done. "Move to the second and subsequent duties," he said, "only after you have completed the first." Later the president said that this one idea revolutionized his whole executive team—the members of which had all been instructed to use the idea for two weeks.

You, too, can become an efficiency expert in all that you do if you'll believe this advice from men who have tried and proved it to be very successful. For instance, my wife even set up her schedule for housework based on this twenty-five-thousand-dollar idea. Her schedule hangs on the inside of a kitchen-cupboard door, and it tells her what must be done each day of the week and in what order.

In chapter nine, we talked about setting up a schedule that tells you at a glance those things that you should do every day of the week. Be sure to refer to this schedule when making up your plan for each day's work. In other words, mix the new items of work for today with those regular duties and rearrange them all so that they are listed and numbered in the order of importance. That's how you establish the one-two-three system. The sheet I use for my daily planning is shown in Figure Six.

Though I've mentioned already that you should never try to do two or three jobs at once, it bears repeating. When you are determined to do one job at a time, the law of accumulation goes to work for you. That law was explained by Isaiah when he wrote: "For precept must be upon precept, precept upon precept; line upon line, line upon line; here a little, and there a little" (Isaiah 28:10). It's the law that says, "Faithfulness to each part of the job will accomplish great things." Richard Cecil, an English divine of the eighteenth century, understood this law. "The shortest way to do many things," he said, "is to do only one thing at a time."

Doing one thing at a time, however, should not prevent you from the important time-saving practice of grouping or packaging your duties. For example, study your list to see if certain duties are related by nature. If you package all those so related, you'll gain a continuity in your work—a continuity that will prevent you from wasting time by repeatedly changing the nature of what you are doing. For example, don't read your incoming letters and memos at one time and answer them at another time. These two jobs are intimately related and should go together. Telephone calls should be grouped together and made all at the same time.

Once you have established this one-two-three system for getting through the day as a habit of life, you'll be so pleased with the effect it has on your work that you'll look forward to each day with the enthusiasm of the psalmist who wrote: "This is the day

Things to Do Today

Date _____   Completed

1 _____   _____

2 _____   _____

3 _____   _____

4 _____   _____

5 _____   _____

6 _____   _____

7 _____   _____

8 _____   _____

9 _____   _____

10 _____   _____

11 _____   _____

12 _____   _____

Notes

Figure 6

which the Lord hath made; we will rejoice and be glad in it"
(Psalms 118:24). And you'll be able to answer in the affirmative
the questions in these lines by an unknown poet:

> Did you waste the day, or use it?
> Was it well or poorly spent?
> Did you leave a trail of kindness,
> Or a scar of discontent?
> As you close your eyes in slumber,
> Do you think your God can say,
> "You have earned one more tomorrow
> By the work you did today"?

11

Write Your Way to More Time

As far as time management is concerned, the area of communication can be a danger area. Unless this part of your work is well controlled, much of your valuable time will be wasted. Because of this, it is imperative that you recognize the importance of knowing how to communicate your ideas to others. Effective leadership depends largely on successful communications. For example, you should know that there are several methods for getting your message across and that your choice of method depends on the person or persons you are trying to reach and upon the nature of your message.

Here are some of the methods to choose from: letter, memo, telegram, bulletin, news release, advertisement, article, telephone, or personal interview. If you want to reach a large number of persons, you might use the method the Lord suggested to Habakkuk: ". . . Write the vision, and make it plain upon tables, that he may run that readeth it" (Habakkuk 2:2). The idea apparently was to put the message in large writing in a public place, where one could read it at a glance, easily remember it, and thus be enabled to convey it to his neighbors. Ken Taylor's paraphrase in the Living Bible, I think, catches this meaning a little more clearly: ". . . Write my answer on a billboard, large and clear, so that anyone can read it at a glance and rush to tell the others."

Much of the writing, especially letter writing, by business and church leaders does not follow that good biblical advice for effective communication. It is not easily read, usually it's too wordy, and often it's too stiff and formal. For some reason, I guess it's an unconfessed fear of writing, most people forget the way they speak when they pick up a pen to write. Yet the best writing, if it were possible, would be much like conversation on paper.

Those who spend their lives making a study of these things say that most letters are about 75 percent redundant, and that they would be greatly improved in clarity and received more readily by having their content cut to 25 percent. To do this is not only better communications, but it indicates that the writer is a person of knowledge. Solomon confirmed this when he said, "He that hath knowledge spareth his words . . ." (Proverbs 17:27).

Have you ever sat in church, listening to a soloist trying to sing a voice instead of a message? There are leaders like that: They write to display their vocabularies, in an attempt to impress their readers. For example, before me on my desk, as I write this, lies a Christian magazine opened to an article by a church pastor. This magazine is intended for the average church member, but I will venture to say that not 10 in each 100 readers would get anything from the article in question. Here are some of the phrases he used in his first three paragraphs: *fundamental orthodoxy, radical theology, undeniable phenomenon, primary thread of commonality, this helical web, empiricists, classical liberalism,* and then he writes that some of this might be an "oversimplification." It was a critical article, of course, and the writer, in an attempt to judge his selected targets, used these words from Proverbs 16:18: "Pride goeth before destruction, and an haughty spirit before a fall."

He seemed to have closed his mind to the fact that his own writing was a proud and pompous attempt to impress others with his vocabulary and knowledge.

Another mistake in his article, which one sees so often in amateur writing, was his constant reference to himself as "this writer." It smacks of pomposity to call oneself *this writer*. It is far better writing to say *I* or *me*.

Then there's the false humility attempted by the writer who uses the editorial *we* in his writing. Some go to such extremes with this that the result is ridiculous. Here's a sample of this from a student pastor's report: "We prepared for visitation that stormy morning, kissed our wife good-bye, and went out into the blizzard, where we froze our left ear before we made the first call, about five miles from where we live." Mark Twain once said, "Only presidents, editors, and people with tapeworm have the right to use the editorial *we*." And Rudolf Flesch, that master teacher of *Plain Talk*, says that he would demote even editors to a plain, ordinary *I*.

Getting rid of these common flaws in writing, however, isn't enough. To be an effective communicator, one must learn how to plan and complete a piece of writing. I think this bit of advice on how to be an effective public speaker is equally applicable to writing: "Be brief, be bright, be gone." Be careful, however, in your attempts to "be brief" and "be gone." It is possible to say too little and leave your reader confused about your meaning. And "be bright" does not mean to use words and styles that make you look bright. It means to know what you intend to write about before you write.

Every piece of good nonfiction writing uses the following four-step formula: get attention, arouse interest, create confidence and desire, stir to action. A student at the University of Oklahoma school of writing reduced this formula to four simple words that I have used ever since I first heard them. They are: *hey, you, see, so.* These four steps stick to the thought processes of every normal mind, and you should memorize them right now if you want to be a better writer and speaker. Let's look at an example of this formula at work. You'll find it in 2 Chronicles 2:11–16, where Huram, the king of Tyre, sends a letter in answer to Solomon's request for skilled artisans and building supplies for the temple he intends to build for God. To get Solomon's attention (*hey*) and interest (*you*) Huram writes:

". . . Because the Lord hath loved his people, he hath made thee king over them" (2 Chronicles 2:11). He then goes on to honor Solomon's God as the Creator, to call Solomon the wise son of David who is "endued with prudence and understanding," and then voices his confidence that Solomon will "build an house for the Lord . . ." (2 Chronicles 2:12).

He creates confidence and desire (*see*) for what he is offering, by getting down to cases; he substantiates the skill and reliability of the artisan he is sending; he refuses the payment offered him by Solomon; and he explains how he'll get the supplies to the seaport of Joppa.

He then makes a bid for action (*so*) when he writes ". . . and thou shalt carry it up to Jerusalem" (2 Chronicles 2:16).

You can apply this four-step formula to everything you write. Instead of writing the usual boring business letter, try your hand at using this formula to liven up your correspondence. For example, I once got a letter from a magazine editor to tell me he had accepted an article of mine for publication.

"Dear Mr. Bowman," he wrote, "Does this letter feel warm? It should if it reflects how we feel about your piece, which we are going to feature in a forthcoming issue of our publication."

In those few words, he had my undivided attention and keen interest. There was no doubt that I would continue to read the rest of that letter. And that's the essence of all good writing—*continuity*. If your reader stops reading, you are out of a job as a writer. If you use the *hey, you, see, so* formula as you plan a piece of writing, you can then take advantage of odd moments to do some of the actual writing. Novelist John Erskine learned the value of this and spoke of his surprise at the results.

Whenever I had five unoccupied minutes, I sat down and wrote a hundred words or so. To my astonishment, at the end of the week I had a sizeable manuscript ready for revision. Later on I wrote novels by the same piecemeal method.

It is easy to see that the professional writer knows how to link his work with the clock and write his way to more time. You can do the same if you'll adopt the suggestions made in this chapter. Now, before I close this chapter, here are a few more helpful hints for the person who wants to be a better writer: Make it a habit to write something every day. Try to scribble a few hundred words of original composition early in the morning before you read the mail or take a look at the morning newspaper. Keep a notebook in your pocket or pocketbook and use it to jot down ideas that come to you through the day. Place it on your night table so that you can capture those great thoughts you have during the night. Regardless of what you do—pastor, leader, manager, doctor, lawyer—you can increase your ministry to Christ and to others by becoming a better writer. You'll gain more time, too.

12

Beware of Excessive Involvement

When I was a manager in the business world, the vice-president of our company once introduced me to a friend of his by saying, "This is George Bowman. He doesn't do too bad a job for us, when you consider that he gives us only about twenty-five percent of his time." His percentage guess wasn't far off the mark, because I had become so involved in outside activities that they were eating up far more time than I was giving to my regular job.

For example, at that time, besides my work as a manager, I was trying to fill the following positions: Bible-class teacher, church deacon and secretary-treasurer, editor of two nonprofit publications, president of a national writers' association, and I was giving between 75 and 100 public talks a year. Later, I realized that while trying to serve others I had spread myself too thin. Though no one ever complained about the quality of my work, I know now that much of it was not done as well as it might have been. With honest motives and good intentions, I had made the mistake of substituting quantitative activity for qualitative work. From that experience I learned how easy it is to slide into a state of excessive involvement.

No one can expect to be an efficient manager of his time and work when he is so extensively committed. In fact, excessive involvement is caused by the failure to manage one's time and the failure to prepare one's work. For example, your time, energy, and abilities should be matched up in a workable combination with your family responsibilities, your employment obligations, and your duties to church and community. Please note the phrase "workable combination," because that phrase represents the only way you can avoid excessive involvement.

But creating a workable combination is not an easy task, because there are far more demands for leadership than there are leaders. Anyone with the ability to lead a group will receive many invitations to get involved in the administrative work of churches, Bible societies, missions, service clubs, schools, hospitals, and charity drives. It's not always easy to say no to such demands, but that is one of the essential elements in the workable combination that prevents excessive involvement. You must know when to say no.

Some persons become victims of excessive involvement right on the job. A corporation executive once said, "A high-salaried employee has no right to complain about long hours or about taking work home. That's what he's being paid for." But that executive was wrong. No employee should be expected to work so hard that he has little or no time for his family, church, and community. That kind of pressure creates compulsive workers, and compulsive workers make very poor managers. It is possible to so drive yourself that you turn into a *workaholic*—one who ceases to enjoy his leisure time.

There's a trend today toward shorter work weeks, longer vacations, and earlier retirement. Predictions are that it won't be long before we'll work only four days a week, go on five-week vacations, and retire on pension at age sixty. If you haven't learned to enjoy your leisure time, such changes will only add to your frustrations and provide you with more free time not to enjoy. Psychologists and sociologists have come up with some solutions to this problem of being bored by free time.

Boredom is part of life, they say, and we should recognize its inevitability. To overcome boredom during leisure time, they suggest that you "act childish" and "be a daydreamer." As for me, I would find no alleviation from boredom in those three "solutions." I don't think that I have to accept boredom as a way of life, for the Bible tells me that I can, through a proper faith relationship to Christ, learn to be content whatever my circumstances. To accept boredom as an inevitable part of my life is to give in to a wrong and sinful attitude. Believers in Jesus Christ have been raised to a victory position in their Lord, and to them, the Bible says, "Set your affection on things above, not on things on the earth" (Colossians 3:2).

The advice to "act childish" suggests that restraints lead to unhappiness and boredom. Nothing could be farther from the truth. The Bible teaches it, and experience proves it, that the controlled life is the happy life. To abandon oneself to childishness is to seek freedom and satisfaction by abandoning oneself to his whims and fancies. H. A. Overstreet, in his book, *The Mature Mind,* quotes Denis Diderot as saying "All children are essentially criminal. It is merely our good luck that their physical powers are still too limited to permit them to carry out their destructiveness." Overstreet then says that Diderot might have expanded his remarks by saying, "All childish minds are dangerous, but particularly when those minds are housed in adult bodies."

For a grown-up person to act childish, then, is a method too dangerous to use as a relief from boredom; the results could be disastrous. And the advice to "be a daydreamer" isn't much better, for it encourages a false escape route from reality—an escape route that circles right back to the problem of being bored with leisure time when the "dreamer" wakes up.

Those who are bored by free time can't really say that they enjoy their work, to which they have become captives. It is not biblical to spend every waking hour on the job. While there are many admonitions to work, there are plenty of exhortations to rest. Jesus once said, ". . . Come ye yourselves apart into a desert place, and rest a while . . ." (Mark 6:31). In today's manner of speaking, that means, "Get away from the crowd. Don't allow yourself to be imprisoned by your work, but learn to get alone with God in a private place, for they that wait upon the Lord shall renew their strength for the battle of life."

If one doesn't enjoy his work and is bored with his leisure time, what has he got to live for? The truth of the matter is that he likely doesn't enjoy life. For such a person there is no successful plan for the management of his time. Finding it unpleasant to put in time, he would regard it as unthinkable to plan the unpleasant. Perhaps he doesn't enjoy life because he is always trying to avoid taking risks. He could change all that by accepting the fact that risks are a part of living and that they furnish one with challenges that can be exciting and enjoyable.

Perhaps he's unhappy about life because he constantly worries about his health or his family or his work or his money. There is no way that such a worrywart could be a good time manager.

When you set out to create that workable combination of the factors in your life, don't forget that planning your time is determined by elimination as much as it is by assimilation. You must be determined to get rid of any activity or work habit that borders on excess and that adds to an already heavy work load. I once read that a college president said that the first qualification for leadership is a wastebasket.

Leadership also learns to pace itself. The leader who runs around looking as though he hasn't a minute to spare reminds me of that bit of traffic-police advice to automobile drivers: "They called him Speedy for short, but not for long." Being too busy can cause you to overlook the essential part of your job, like the man in the days of King Ahab of Israel, who lost a prisoner of war he had been commanded to keep. His excuse to the king was, "And as thy servant was busy here and there, he [the prisoner] was gone . . ." (1 Kings 20:40).

Yes, it is easy to become so busy—so excessively involved—that life is no longer enjoyed. Don't allow this to happen to you. Create that workable combination in which you match your time, energy, and abilities with your duties, by doing the things suggested in this chapter. Here is a summary of those suggestions:

Say no to activities that will upset your time balance.

Don't allow your work to put you in prison. If you control your job instead of its controlling you, you'll never be bored by your work.

Learn to enjoy life, with all its risks and challenges, as exciting and pleasurable.

Learn the value of getting away from it all once in a while, not to waste time, but to renew strength through rest and prayer.

Learn to be content with your lot in life as God's appointment for you and as the environment where He expects you to serve Him.

Delegate as much of your detail work as you can. If you can't
learn to do this, you're not yet a leader.

Don't be led by non-Christian counselors to take false escape
routes from reality.

Use that philosophical "wastebasket" and get rid of
anything—even some responsibilities—that hinders you
from a full enjoyment of your work, your family, your
church, and your neighborhood.

Stop rushing around—to hurry doesn't necessarily save time.

Don't mix business with your personal life, such as evenings at
home or meals in a restaurant. Take time to relax—every
day.

Remember that you have a victory position in Jesus Christ.

13

Reading With a System

It is impossible to read the Bible without discovering that wisdom and research belong together. Knowledgeable leaders who want to lead others to greater heights of learning and accomplishment know how to gather, systematize, and present information in an acceptable fashion. The Holy Spirit of God speaks of this subject when He says:

> And moreover, because the preacher was wise, he still taught the people knowledge; yea, he gave good heed, and sought out, and set in order many proverbs. The preacher sought to find out acceptable words: and that which was written was upright, even words of truth.
>
> Ecclesiastes 12:9, 10

True success as a leader is not what some people think it is—a soft job with nothing to do but give orders to subordinates. Consequently, many seek to be leaders without any comprehension of the constant reading and research a leader must do to be successful. The reading and research is necessary because, without it, a leader could not perform one of the major functions of leadership: decision making.

If you are in the position to have the last word in making a decision, you must not try to play "hot potato" with your associates—that is, tossing the responsibility for making the decision back and forth like a hot potato. That kind of thing causes many wrong decisions to be made and forces you to do a lot of backtracking to cover up faulty judgments. If you want to make wise decisions that produce results, you must follow the steps outlined in the Bible passage quoted above.

You must "give good heed." That is, you must be a student of all the literature germane to your work.

You must "seek out." That is, you must know how to glean the important ideas from what you read.

You must "set in order." That is, you must learn how to systematize your ideas for effective use.

You must "find out acceptable words." That is, you must learn how to communicate your conclusions to others.

While the Bible does say that ". . . much study is a weariness of the flesh" (Ecclesiastes 12:12), leaders must accept reading as an important part of their job. That job is not easy, but if you can learn to love reading and research, much of the weariness will disappear. A mark of the true leader, then, is a thirst for information. But his problem is: "How do I tie all this reading and research into my plan to budget time?"

The first step in a program of reading and research is to plan time for reading every day. This should be fitted into your planning calendar, along with your other duties, because, for a leader, reading is one of the most important duties he performs. Larston

Farrar, free-lance writer of note, once said, "I read at least four hours a day, on an average, year in and year out. Still I feel very uninformed about what is going on in this broad world and I am constantly seeking new sources of valid information."

Note that phrase "valid information," for it is the key to the second step in your plan of reading and research. That step is to weed out irrelevant reading material. Even if some reading is enjoyable, don't waste your time on it if it does not provide you with valid information to help you do a better job at work, at home, at church, or in your community.

The third step is the most important one. Learn to read with this objective: to get the valid information at one reading, and to be able to find those relevant passages at any time in the future.

To accomplish this objective, you must read everything with a pen or pencil in your hand and have no hesitation about marking everything you read. If the book or magazine is not yours, of course, you'll not be able to mark it, but you can take notes of what you would have marked had the book or magazine been yours.

Let's start with how to read a book. Every informative book is written to a plan, and you can find that plan by reading the table of contents, the preface, and the introduction. Read these first to learn the author's purpose and to select only those chapters which are relevant to your work.

After you have selected the chapters you want to read, turn to the first one of your choice and read the first paragraph. Now stop and underline the central idea in that paragraph. Try to underline as few words as possible. If you can't find the central idea stated in a few words, go to the margin and write out the central idea of that paragraph in your own words. Next read paragraph two and mark its central idea and then take a second to reread the two central ideas before you read the third paragraph.

Continue this process right through all the passages you have chosen to read. And don't forget to reread the underlined words in all the previous paragraphs before you go on to the next paragraph. Once you have marked a book in this way, you can return to it at any time and simply read those underlined words to get a grasp of the whole. In just a few minutes, you can gallop through the central ideas of an entire book. If you make this method of reading a fixed habit, you can become an expert on any subject you care to study.

James Garfield, twentieth president of the U.S.A., once said, "Ideas control the world." Anything with that much power must itself be put under control. Without some kind of system to manage our ideas, their power could run amok and cause us irreparable harm. For instance, think of the time wasted when ideas are not systematized. I have found that my idea filing system saves me hundreds of hours each year.

If you want to build such a system for yourself, start by organizing all your books according to subject. If all your books on business are in one place, you will save time when you want to look up an idea on any business subject. If your section on business is large, organize all your business books by subtopics in alphabetical order. Beginning at the left of your business shelf, place your books in this order:

Business handbooks of general information
Accounting and commercial law
Banking
Buying techniques
Corporations
Correspondence
Ethics

Financing and promotion
Investments
Machines and equipment
Management
Marketing
Personnel
Salesmanship
Success stories

Some persons recommend that books be stored alphabetically by titles or by authors. Accept neither recommendation, and file your books by subject alone. You can do the same with magazine and newspaper articles you want to keep. Sort them into subjects, and place them in a file folder clearly marked by that subject. If you want to go a step farther in control of ideas, set up a loose-leaf notebook with a page for each subject on which you have material filed. By numbering the clippings and indicating those numbers on your loose-leaf sheets, you need look only at the sheet to find what you have in a folder. Ideas from your books could also be listed on the sheets. The important thing is that the loose-leaf sheet should tell you quickly where to find the item you are looking for. (*See* Figure Seven.)

You can use this same system to file all your own public talks and any articles you write for publication. The subjects you use will depend on your interests and work. According to one filing expert, there are only forty-three major subjects in the world, so if you wanted to file clippings on all of them, without a subtopic breakdown, you'd need only forty-three folders to start.

Shy away from an elaborate filing system. Make sure that you

Filing Index Sheet

Subject _____

Publication	Date	Number	Remarks

Figure 7

obey the basic laws or guiding principles for a good idea file and keep it as simple as you can. Those laws are:

Anticipation:	Looking ahead
Designation:	Classify by topics
Simplicity:	Work for instant recall
Conformity:	Don't break away from your plan
Timeliness:	Don't procrastinate any part of the filing process
Function:	Don't waste time on anything that does not serve your objective
Fulfillment:	You must be happy with the result

In my own system I have several large index binders, now with thousands of items listed on their pages, some of which were entered twenty years ago. These items are to be found in books, on tapes, in clippings, notebooks, my own speech and article manuscripts, and on cards in a smaller file. I can recall any item from any of those sources within a minute or less. By filing only the items I have read or listened to (those on tape), I can quickly refresh my memory on what I've studied on any given subject, in preparation for writing an article or giving a speech. I have found it to be an invaluable system for the man who wants to save time.

14

Visitors and the Telephone

The pressure of unplanned visits and uncontrolled telephone calls can become so great that you'll not only waste much of your time, but you may develop a wrong attitude toward people. To avoid this, you should constantly remember that Christians have a biblical law for dealing with others.

"Therefore all things whatsoever ye would that men should do to you," said Jesus, "do ye even so to them: for this is the law . . ." (Matthew 7:12).

When the American Management Association made a survey of how executives used their time, "too much talk" was their most common complaint. They had to attend too many meetings, they said, sit in on many unwanted interviews, and handle too many telephone calls. A large number of executives used only one word to name their big grievance: *telephone.*

There's no doubt about it, the telephone caller can be one of our biggest time wasters. "For some people," an associate of mine used to say, "picking up the receiver is their cue to open up a fountain of verbiage that just about drives a busy man, not only

113

up the wall, but right over the top." Wouldn't it be great if callers would abide by the divine counsel that says there's ". . . a time to keep silence, and a time to speak"? (Ecclesiastes 3:7.)

But such is not the case, and it is left up to you, as the executive or leader, to put some control on how you handle callers. First you have to classify your calls and then decide how you're going to put in a system of telephone control for each classification. Telephone calls can come from your family, from your superiors, from your clientele (or from your church members, if you're a pastor), from your friends, and from salesmen.

If you discover that either one or all of these are eating up too much of your time, here are a few suggestions that should help to alleviate the situation: Family members should be told not to call you during business hours, unless there's a family emergency. Most family business can and should be conducted while you are at home.

If one of your superiors telephones you, take the call, unless you are tied up with someone in your office, who came by appointment. Many times a call from your boss will provide you with information that will save you time. If you work for people, however, who are constantly making telephone calls just to chat, you should diplomatically tell them that you like to schedule all your work each day—even to the time you spend on the phone.

When it comes to calls from customers, clientele, or from members of the church for which you are the pastor, it becomes a little more difficult to put in a method of control. If you have a secretary, she should be trained to handle many of your calls without disturbing you. The other day, when I asked a busy pastor if he used priority planning for each day's work, he answered, "Oh, yes, but I don't always follow through. The telephone, you know."

One way to get around this problem is to let people know that there are certain times during the day that you are not available to receive calls. If you must answer the telephone yourself, you can arrange a regular respite from calls by installing one of those private message recorders or signing up for a telephone answering service. The recorder answers your telephone by using a recorded message from you, in which you ask the caller to leave his name and number for you to call when you are free. When cost is a factor, you'll find that such a recorder is much cheaper than a secretary or the telephone answering service.

Another way to cut down on the number of nonproductive calls you receive is this: Make it apparent to such callers that you are far too busy to spend your working day in such profitless exercise. This can be done when you are visiting socially with a group which might include such callers.

"My work load is so heavy these days," you might say within their hearing, "that I've stopped taking telephone calls from my own family during business hours."

Are you the kind of person who, like me, works from his own home? If you are, I suggest that you set up a room as an office that looks different from any other room in the house. You can hardly adopt a businesslike attitude toward your work while you lounge on a sofa in pajamas and housecoat. When you are in your office, act as though you are at work and let your family handle your telephone calls. If there are teenagers in the home, most of the calls will be for them, anyway.

You'll find it easy to train your wife or teenager to pick up the phone and handle calls you don't want to take. "My husband is very busy right now," your wife can say. "If you leave your number, he'll call you when he's free."

Whenever a salesman calls, find out right away what he is selling. If you have no interest, cut the conversation short, for to do so benefits him as well as you. This can be done kindly and with a short word of encouragement to help him on his way.

You can help yourself a great deal, too, by holding your calls until you have time to phone them all one after the other. In other words, manage your other duties so that you leave time to make return calls to those who might get impatient. Ward off repeat calls by never saying something like, "Call me sometime," or, "Give me a call anytime." A busy man cannot afford to make such statements.

Your telephone can be a big time waster, but it can also be a major time-saver. One way you can save a lot of time is to use your telephone to make appointments with those who want to visit your office. This is important, because your visitors, like telephone callers, can ruin your whole day if their visits have not been planned by you.

When you make an appointment on the phone, it is a good idea to establish the purpose of the visit. If you don't, you might be surprised by a problem that will take more time than you can afford. Here, for example, are the five main reasons people will come to see you:

To get information
To be counseled
To give information
To comply with your invitation
To socialize

By establishing on the phone the purpose of the visit, you can sometimes avoid a personal interview. For example, not long ago, I did a story on a busy pastor, and after it was written I telephoned him for an appointment to have him check the manuscript before it was sent away for publication. "Would it save you some time," he asked, "if I just listen to you read it to me over the phone?"

It not only saved my time, but his question was his way of avoiding an unnecessary personal interview. Meetings of committees can be avoided in this way, too. If there's only a bit of business to attend to, a few phone calls by the chairman can give him a consensus of opinion on which he can make a decision to be ratified at the next meeting.

When a visitor comes to your office by appointment, another good time-saving technique is to have an understanding about the amount of time available for his visit. You can do this tactfully by saying that you do not allow telephone calls during personal interviews, and you'd like to tell your secretary how long to hold your calls. Or you might tell him that you have another visitor coming to see you at a certain time (if that is true), or that you have a project that must be started at a definite time. When the time allotted for your visitor is up, you can stand up, come around in front of your desk, thank him for coming, and reach out to shake hands.

The whole idea here is to show a genuine interest in your visitor and never to make the mistake of letting your control reveal itself in formality or officiousness. In the light of the law in Matthew 7:12, there is no room in the life of a Christian leader for being rude or officiously brusque.

Then there's the visitor who likes to gossip about fellow employees. You can handle this by asking him to wait until you call in the person he's talking about to hear what he has to say. "It wouldn't be right for you and me to talk about him behind his back," you can suggest. "So, if you don't mind, I'd like him to sit in on our conversation." That will not only stop the gossip during that visit, but you'll never hear gossip from him again.

And how about the I-am-important visitor? You know, the chap who thinks his time is many times more important than yours and demands to see you. Such people are usually important only in their own eyes, and their attitude should not be encouraged. If you think there is any hope for improvement in such a visitor, take the time to tell him the kind of impression he is creating and make a few suggestions about how he can be far more effective in his particular position—especially in the way he deals with people. Don't be shocked, however, if your advice is spurned, because most self-important persons are possessed by prejudice, the iron curtain of the mind, and you'll discover that it's hard to penetrate.

Most leaders have a hard time overcoming the temptation to play favorites with members of their staffs. You see, rightly defined, success is "lonely responsibility," and it is very easy for a man in such a position to seek companionship with those on his staff whose personalities are compatible with his. It is the same for pastors in their relationship with church officers and members.

Make a member of your staff a favorite, and you'll lose the respect of all the rest. Be on friendly terms with all those with whom you deal, but don't ever become too chummy with any one or two people. Such favoritism stands out like a red light and causes people's hearts to burn with envy. If you are too gregarious to put up with the loneliness of true leadership, don't aspire to a position in which you are called upon to supervise others.

Communication control is not an easy skill to acquire, and this is especially true for the leader. Not that he can't speak in public or engage in an intelligent conversation, but it is very difficult for the man who knows the solution to sit back quietly while a member of his staff struggles with a problem.

You must learn to do this, however, or your staff member will never acquire the skill to solve problems on his own. Knowing you can do a job in a few minutes which will take your staff member several hours to complete, as a true leader you'll exercise patience, because you want your employee to share in the blessings of personal development.

Perhaps James was speaking about this kind of thing when he said, ". . . let every man be swift to hear, slow to speak, slow to wrath" (James 1:19).

Which brings us to the subject of what to do when an argument arises because of a difference of opinion between you and an associate in your work. A simple rule to follow is this: Seek not to win an argument, but to win the person. Dale Carnegie once coined a beautiful argument-killing response to the person who made some insulting or antagonistic remark.

"I don't blame you one iota for feeling the way you do," he would say. "For if I were you, I would undoubtedly feel the same."

No one can rationally go on arguing when you agree with him, especially when the agreement, as it is phrased above, is the truth. You see, if you were the man who had insulted you, you would feel the same as he—would you not? The Apostle Paul knew about this way of dealing with others, and here's how he put it: "Let your speech be alway with grace, seasoned with salt, that ye may know how ye ought to answer every man" (Colossians 4:6).

15

Life Is Not Measured by Time

Most of our trouble with the whole process of trying to manage our time comes from our wrong ideas about time and how we are related to it. For instance, don't you find that your experience of time is determined by your attitude toward what you are doing? When you are engaged in an activity that makes you excited and enthusiastic, don't you experience a feeling that time is racing by? On the other hand, if you have been forced into performing a task that you resent, doesn't the time seem to drag?

Psychologists tell us that our experience of time and our memories can also be affected by, and are subject to, illusions. For example, have you ever gotten up in the morning complaining that you hadn't slept all night? According to psychologists, it is likely that you were awake for only a short time during the night, but that experience left you with an illusion that you had been awake for a much longer time.

Our physical condition can also affect our ideas about time. Tests have proved that a change in body temperature can change one's conception of time, and the taking of any kind of drugs (medicinal or illegal) can create wrong impressions of how we are experiencing time.

This happens, too, in the case of the person who allows himself to be hypnotized. He can be put to sleep for a few minutes, and, while under hypnosis, can be convinced that he was asleep for hours or days. This is also true of the person who is deeply impressed by another's strong personality. For example, think of the last time you spent two or three hours with someone who really captivated your whole attention. Did you not feel that the two or three hours went by as though they were just a few minutes?

While we cannot escape having our ideas about time influenced by attitudes, illusions, and physical conditions, we can recognize that this goes on and thus be in a better position to understand time and how to control it. Eric Von Daniken, author of *Gods From Outer Space,* says, ". . . time can be manipulated by speed and energy." Though he was speaking of the time-dilating theory in space travel, his remark points to the idea that we *do* have some control over the way time is used in our own lives.

Think, for example, of the man who feels he has a long time to live and conducts himself accordingly. Enjoying life to the fullest, he may neglect to get busy with the things he wants to do with his life. Suddenly he'll wake up to the fact that his attitude has put him in a state of suspended animation over the conveyor belt of accomplishment and that he's so far behind that he'll never be able to catch up to where he should have been with his work.

It's too bad that so many people can't learn an essential truth about life without going through that kind of experience. That essential truth is this: Life is not measured by the years we live, but by what worthwhile things we accomplish during those years. You can see this when you study the biographies of great men and women.

For example, George Whitefield is not remembered because he lived fifty-six years, but because of his work. He traveled through England, Scotland, and America, preaching as none had ever done before. His approximately eighteen thousand sermons were used of God to win tens of thousands to faith in Jesus Christ. As J. C. Ryle once said, "I have come to the conclusion that Whitefield was one of the most powerful and extraordinary preachers the world has ever seen." The only important part his years play in his biography is that he was able to accomplish so much in such a short time!

It is far better to die young and have accomplished something worthwhile in life than to live to 100 and have done nothing. There is nothing in the Bible about receiving a reward for living a long life. Even the mercy of God, according to David, is linked with man's accountability for his deeds, not his years. "Also unto thee, O Lord, belongeth mercy: for thou renderest to every man according to his work" (Psalms 62:12).

The way some people talk, you'd think that leisure was the most important thing in life. They spend all year planning their vacation. I think it was Calvin Coolidge, the thirtieth president of the U.S.A., who said, "Work is the main function of life." And our attitude toward work will determine our success or failure in life. So don't think of life in terms of years on a calendar or hours on a clock, but in terms of the little verse that says: "Only one life; 'twill soon be past; Only what's done for Christ will last."

Perhaps my fellow-Canadian author J. H. Hunter put it best when he said, "We live in deeds, not years, in feelings, not in figures on a dial."

No one plans to waste his life; it just happens. But here is how it happens: the life waster lines up all his self-styled values of life: ambition, wealth, pleasure, popularity, and leisure. Then, making major time contributions to them, he puts the most important value—worthwhile achievement—at the end of the line. An up-to-date example of this kind of thing is the late Elvis Presley, who gave his whole life to the wild sexuality of rock music. Several years before he died, the sparkle of popularity had been dimmed by sickness, fear, and seclusion. His physique had been weakened by drugs and indolence; and the spirit that had made him ambitious for fame and pleasure had gone out of him. Listen to him speaking about himself: "Sometimes when I'm in a crowd a kind of inner loneliness will suddenly strike me, for no reason. I can't explain it. It seldom happens in the mornings, but many afternoons, when I slow down, I'm very lonely." Once, while looking at the crowds of fans milling around his gate, he said, "I'm a prisoner. I have all the money in the world and I can't go beyond those gates."

How pathetic it is to witness the disintegration of one who has never learned that life is measured only by worthwhile achievement. How much better it would be for all of us if we would remember that when God tests a man, He does so by looking at his direction and his production. Here's how Jeremiah recorded God's Word on this: "I the Lord search the heart, I try the reins, even to give every man according to his ways, and according to the fruit of his doings" (17:10).

I have tried in this book to adhere to its theme that we should live our lives with the clear understanding that every one of us shall give account of himself to God. I wanted to convince myself and you that the great objective in life is to glorify God and to enjoy Him forever. I deliberately refused to paint an exciting picture of men and women finding it an easy thing to succeed at managing their time and work. Refusing to hold or to write about wrong conceptions of life and work and time, I've tried to tell you the truth about those things, as I see it. Consequently, I must confess that I believe we'll never get a true picture of life until we ". . . all appear before the judgment seat of Christ . . ." (2

Corinthians 5:10). Martin Luther explained it better than I when he said:

> Here on earth we can form no conception of this life for it passes on piecemeal, so to speak, foot by foot, to the Last Day. But before God it all stands in one moment . . . . The first man is just as near to Him as the one who shall be born last.

The Bible is filled with the truth that man cannot escape his responsibilities to God and to others. To attempt such an escape is to take the road to sure destruction. This is just as true of nations as it is of people. For example, here is historian Edith Hamilton on her favorite subject, Greece: "When the freedom they wished for most was freedom from responsibility, then Athens ceased to be free and was never free again."

The greatest freedom of all is to accept one's responsibility for the Gospel of Jesus Christ. That responsibility includes that we believe what the Bible says about us: That we have been ruined by the Fall and that we suffer from a natural corruption of heart. It also includes the recognition of our need to be born again by the regenerating work of the Holy Spirit. This work reveals itself in our willingness to repent (turn away) from our sin and to put our faith in Jesus Christ—the only source of redemption and complete justification before God. That responsibility also includes that we strive to live up to our dead-to-sin position in Christ and that we have no right to profess that position apart from a holy life. It was to irresponsible professors of faith in Christ—those to whom He had been teaching the principle of continuing faith—that the Lord spoke these words: "If the Son therefore shall make you free, ye shall be free indeed" (John 8:36).

Many professing Christians do not have this freedom, because they refuse to measure their lives by worthwhile achievement. In their minds and in their lives they have come to believe that faith for a moment means life for eternity. They have made the mistake of separating faith from works and have sought to justify that mistake by saying that salvation is not by works.

What they have failed to see is that saving faith is not a passive attitude of mind. Nowhere in the Bible is faith ever linked with inactivity. It is always shown as an ongoing, progressive conviction of heart that motivates a life of holiness. I am not saying that we are saved by works, but that we are saved by a faith that works. I am not saying that we are saved by obedience, but that we are saved by an obedient faith. I am convinced that this is the only kind of faith taught in the Bible.

And that takes us back to the central thought of this chapter: The true values of life as well as the quality of faith are measured, not by how many years we live and by what we say we believe, but by what we do. "By their fruits," said Jesus, "ye shall know them."

The one sure way to develop a fruitless life is to look upon the time of your life as a destructive power—something that grays your hair, pales your skin, dulls your hearing, dims your eyesight, bends your back, weakens your legs, shortens your breath, and in the end devours your very life. I used to think of time like that. In fact, I even said something to that effect in one of my books. Today, however, I have a different view of time. I think it is a gift from God that we can use to glorify Him. Rather than thinking of time as a destructive force, you and I should see time as an instrument of sanctification—one of the means by which God enables us to exercise our faith and get victory over our circumstances.

Those who think of time as a destructive power must also be afraid of the chronological process. As Christians, those who have eternal life, we ought not to fear that process. Rather, we ought to recognize the importance of our striving to fill up its limited confines with work that honors God. Isn't that what our Lord Jesus Christ commanded is to do? "Occupy," He said, "till I come" (Luke 19:13).

That word *occupy* means to fill your life with the kind of meaningful activity that glorifies the Saviour's name. To do that, you must learn how to manage your affairs and how to order your time. May the triune God take the ideas in this book and use them to do just that for you. And may you discover the rich joy and the deep satisfaction that comes from a controlled life dedicated to the cause of Christ.